ANTIQUE HOUSEHOLD GADGETS
AND APPLIANCES

Antique Household Gadgets and Appliances

c. 1860 to 1930

David de Haan

BLANDFORD PRESS

POOLE   DORSET

First published in 1977
by Blandford Press Ltd,
Link House, West Street, Poole,
Dorset BH15 1LL

Colour printed by Sackville Press (Billericay) Ltd
Text printed and books bound in Great Britain by
Richard Clay (The Chaucer Press) Ltd
Bungay, Suffolk

Contents

Preface

In preparing the book I have been fortunate in being able to make great use of the technical files and expertise of my friends and colleagues at the Science Museum, London. It is to them I owe the greatest debt. The illustrations have been mainly drawn both from actual objects in the Museum as well as those privately owned (notably by the artists, Elsie Camidge, Mary Cooper, Martin Rickitt, Wendy Meadway, the proprietors of the Chelsea Rendezvous Restaurant and the Author). The other key sources were contemporary literature. These include the mail-order catalogues of the Army and Navy Stores, Gamages, Buck and Hickman, Baird and Tatlock, Sears and Roebuck and the Country Gentleman's Catalogue. Of the many periodicals, I should mention the *Illustrated London News, Scientific American, The Graphic, The Queen, The Ladies' Home Journal* and *Vogue*. Aga Appliances Ltd were also very helpful with reference material. Wendy Gregory helped enormously by typing the manuscript.

Although patent dates are quoted accurately, it must be pointed out that this does not guarantee the gadget or appliance was on sale from that moment onwards. Many items were being sold before their patent applications were submitted, and similarly, other items remained off the market until long after the patent had been granted. They can only offer a helpful guide, so wherever possible I have relied on contemporary advertisements and reviews for dating.

For the sake of neatness I have omitted the present-day equivalent of outdated prices, and offer a table below for those who feel lost:

One guinea (21/–)	£1·05	5/–	25p
£1/–/– (20/–)	£1·00	2/–	10p
17/6	75p	1/– (12d)	5p
10/–	50p	6d.	2½p

Nor have I translated them into a common currency because of the differing exchange rates of different periods. Similarly Imperial measurements have not been converted to their metric equivalent mainly because the gadgets were conceived in Imperial units—a 3-pint kettle was not made as a 1·71-litre kettle!

D de H

Introduction

In Europe the servant classes were common until after the First World War but in America they had become scarce long before. The very way of life with its relatively small population and large acreage had meant hard work and long hours, a receptive environment for any labour-saving device such as a combine harvester, an automobile or a household gadget. After all, if life was unprofitable in one sphere, then you could always leave and try something new, maybe on the expanding western frontier. High wages and shortage of labour produced a ready market for the domestic appliance where the householder wanted his money's worth from his staff or where it was worth his while investing in a machine if it helped persuade the staff to stay. The mood in Europe had been rather different, with the belief prevalent that any easing of the domestic's lot might lead to laziness and bad ways; but by the 1890s this was beginning to change and household gadgets gradually became common.

1

The Kitchen

The kitchen was the centre of the house, the domain of the house-keeper and her helpers, but it was also the meeting-place for all of the staff. Servants were supposed to eat and meet in the Servants' Hall, but more often than not there was no other room to spare and so the kitchen had to serve. Around the large table could be heard all the tales about 'upstairs' and the tedious work that had to be done 'downstairs', the cleaning of pots, pans, silver, plate, curtains, carpets and doorsteps, the running of errands, the changing of beds. With a family consisting of father and mother and four children, it was not uncommon for their pleasant life to be bolstered by the hard work of as many as a dozen servants. For the cook, that was eighteen hungry mouths to feed, so it is not surprising that the kitchen contained the most gadgets in the house. Very few of them, however, were invented by women.

The duties undertaken included not only preparing food, cooking and preserving, but also washing-up, heating water, washing clothes and drying and ironing them, besides catering for an interminable stream of house guests, 'at home' parties and dinner parties. Any gadget that could ease the burden was greatly appreciated.

Cooking

Life in the kitchen centred around cooking. Cast-iron stoves were first available shortly after 1800, but few houses had one until the 1870s so food was cooked as it had been for centuries before on open fires. Pots and kettles hung from adjustable hooks in the chimney and meat was roasted on a spit in front of the fire. The fuel was wood or coal, and would be banked high against the back wall and contained in a fire basket. This had two movable ends which could be cranked in or out depending on the size of joint being roasted. Large kitchens serving guilds, clubs or institutions would have a range of this type wide enough to roast a whole ox, though the heat given out would be enough to roast the cook too, unless a metal screen was provided which had a spy-hole to look through and a slit for a long-handled basting spoon, and of course shelves on the back for keeping food warm.

Some of these large ranges had a smoke-jack which was particularly ingenious as it made use of the heat of the fire to turn the spit. It was done by placing a large horizontal fan or propeller at the point where the chimney narrowed down to a circular shaft. The fan was rotated by the hot air travelling past it, and by a system of simple gears drove several spits, which could be placed at various heights and distances from the fire. The hotter the fire, the faster the spits revolved, but cooking times could be controlled by the position of the spitted roast in relation to the fire. The system, common since 1800, lasted till the early twentieth century. In London, the Skinners Company had an 11-foot-wide range installed as late as 1907 in their Guild Hall kitchen.

Most houses could boast a fire large enough to roast a sucking-pig or a salmon in front of it, but for a smaller joint, the fire ends were cranked together and the meat hung from a hook at the top of a bent metal screen known as a hastener. It had a pan at the bottom for collecting the juices, a hood at the top to keep the heat in the fireplace and a door on the back so the cook could baste the meat. The roast was revolved by a clockwork motor called a bottle-jack, so called because it resembled a bottle. The meat turned first one way and then the other, one complete revolution at a time, and the spring gradually ran down over a period of about half an hour.

The mass-produced cast iron ranges or kitcheners of the 1860s were available in several sizes so as to fit snugly into the fireplaces that had previously housed the open basket, hanging kettles and spits. They still had a section of open fire (and hasteners were still used much later judging by their appearance in Edwardian recipes), but they also had an enclosed oven with a flue built round it, and more often than not a water tank with a capacity of a few gallons (2). This was a great improvement over the endless pans of water on the hob needed just to cope with the washing-up. The larger models (1) had two ovens, from four to six hobs and even a hot-box for warming the plates.

Retailing at up to £16 in 1890, the better ranges included a back-boiler. This was a large tank behind the fire which provided all the domestic hot water, rather than just a couple of washing-ups a day. In the eyes of the manufacturer ranges were marvels; in the eyes of the cook they were treasures, especially for baking; but in the eyes of the over-worked kitchen maid they were the bane of her life. Victorian convention demanded that rather than leave the stove its natural metal colour, it must be gleaming black and shiny every day. But the constant heat of the fire made this rather difficult as it kept burning off the polish, while any bright-work went rusty in the steamy kitchen. Every morning the kitchen maid had to be up before anyone else, sift the ashes and relight the grate (using matches that had been invented in England in 1826, or safety-matches which were a Swedish development of 1855), then put on the kettle for the mistress' early morning tea, but more important, to heat the water so that the household might have a comfortable wash on rising. Then the drudgery began. Using a small cake of stove blacking (which resembled the lead of a pencil), the maid worked it all over the range and then buffed it up with a brush and finally a felt pad. Trade names like 'Zebo', 'Nixey', 'Lion' and 'The Rising Sun' must have become swear words to the poor kitchen maid. For not only did she have the kitchen range to do but also the downstairs fires in the living rooms, the upstairs ones being done by the parlour maid if the house had one. In summer it was not quite so bad, firstly because the fires were not lit, but also because the summer fire bars were bright steel and not the usual black ones. These only required daily rubbing with wire-wool and oil.

The range made the kitchen cozy in winter, but stifling in summer and so the more well-to-do households installed a gas cooker as an auxiliary machine, though there was no question of it replacing the solid-fuel range for a long time. Gas had been used for street lighting in London since 1807 but it was some years after the earliest cooking experiments (which took place in the 1830s) before gas cookers were on sale in 1850. One frightening model was a sheet-metal box covered in wood (*11*). Though we regard this now as a fire hazard, it was common practice in those days to insulate locomotive boilers and steam-engine cylinders with wooden casing, so why not a cooker?

Paraffin made an equally good auxiliary fuel, a popular alternative to wood or coal, particularly in areas with no gas supply. Oil discoveries in Pennsylvania in 1859 brought this new cheap fuel to the American housewife. The heat output of an oil lamp is quite substantial as anyone will know who has accidentally passed his hand too close over the top of the glass chimney, and manufacturers of oil-cooking stoves were quick to exploit this advantage. Ranging in size from the single burner with a long flat wick and trivet above to twin burners serving an oven, plate-warmer and hobs above, paraffin stoves flooded the market from the 1870s to the 1930s (*6,7,8,9*). Being small they had certain disadvantages if you had a lot of mouths to feed, but the convenience and comfort in the hot summer months, not to mention their cheapness, were advantages not to be ignored. The Albionette (*7*) cost less than £2 in 1907.

Returning to gas cookers, early models were rather austere cast iron boxes with a burner at the bottom and a hook at the top. The meat was hung on this hook, as the provision of shelves did not become commonplace until the late 1860s. Up to this time they had been built with only an oven, but by 1866 the familiar multi-burner hotplate was added to the top and the gas cooker became a serious rival to the solid-fuel range (*12*). The problem of a hot-water supply was also solved when B. W. Maughan invented the geyser in 1868. The hard-worked kitchen maid still had the black-leading duties every day, however, because the cooker manufacturers stuck to the convention of using cast iron and bright-work. At least the gas cooker did not produce soot and ashes which was some consolation.

The control taps were usually on the side in early models (*13*), but a more logical approach to space utilisation soon brought them to the front. Improvements in burners appeared in the 1870s with the introduction of air into the pipe producing a more efficient combustion, and ovens were built with a brick lining for better insulation.

4

However, for the next fifty years few major developments affected the layout of the gas cooker until the 1920s when a change in life-style brought about some spectacular alterations.

The large electric motor had released the factory machine from its dependence on the steam engine and so industries could now flourish away from their traditional centres over the coalfields. This meant the opening up of new areas of country with the migration of workers, many of them from domestic posts, to new factories and a rosy future. The First World War had made it clear that women could do the same work as men, political awareness and suffragettes all having had their effect on people's attitude to emancipation. As a result the lady of the house found it increasingly harder to get domestic staff and got more involved, albeit unwillingly, in housework herself. The person that paid for the gadget now actually had to use it, and that produced a much more demanding attitude when it came to value and convenience.

New gas cookers of 1920 had enamelled iron sheets to line the oven, making cleaning much easier. By 1922 the entire cooker had become a lighter unit with enamelled sheets fitted both inside and out, a well insulated double box, efficient, economical and time-saving. Electricity had robbed gas companies of much of their lighting revenue, so greater effort was expended in trying to improve cookers and heaters. In fact the electric light bulb was proving such a success that by 1923 even the gas showrooms had swallowed their pride and gone over to lighting them with electricity. Some cookers became multi-purpose like the Stimex combination gas range of 1920. This not only had the usual oven, grill and boiling rings, but also a built-in hot-water circulator which could provide radiators around the house, and even a gas fire so the poor cook could sit in comfort cooking the dinner and toasting her toes.

A greater improvement followed in 1923 when the flue was moved from the top of the oven to the bottom, thereby reflecting the heat back down on the food before it escaped. At the same time the flue was fitted with a thermostatic control which was called the 'Regulo' by Radiation Ltd., a name which has continued in use to this day. A cookery book was provided with the oven so even the inexperienced

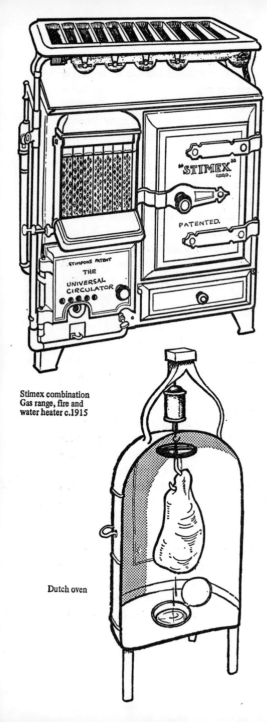

Stimex combination
Gas range, fire and
water heater c.1915

Dutch oven

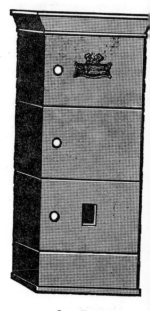

James Sharpe
Gas Cooker 1850

Section drawing of a
'Conover' Electric
Dish Washer 1927

housewife now knew how to produce the desired result, setting the oven temperature exactly right. The old solid fuel range was no match for this model, but for those who did not have gas or electricity salvation was on the way.

The Swedish physicist Gustav Dalen had been experimenting with cookers when an accident robbed him of his sight. A Nobel prizewinner, Dalen went on to develop the perfect solid-fuel cooker which was clean and efficient, and as controllable as the gas cooker. It depended on sound principles of physics, Swedish iron and excellent thermal insulation using Kieselguhr (a heat resistant padding known in the manufacture of explosives since 1867). His cooker, the Aga (4), was invented in 1924. It was thermostatically controlled and also provided circulated hot water to the house. It filled a large gap in the market between the outdated kitcheners and the all-enamel gas cookers, but was not a serious rival to the house in an area served by electricity, which like gas had been developed originally for lighting but had progressed into the areas of heating and cooking.

After a slow start the electric cooker was beginning to be a viable alternative though it had been dogged by prejudice and high prices from the beginning. The first electric oven was Swiss and was used in a hotel which in 1889 had surplus power during the day. Their own waterfall-driven generator provided lighting for the hotel Bernina in Samedan near St Moritz. By 1891 the American firm of Carpenter Electric Heating Manufacturing Co. of St Paul, Minn., were offering electric cookers on sale. Then an electric kitchen was exhibited at the Chicago World Fair of 1893 and in the last few years of the century new electric cooking devices began arousing excitement and receiving plenty of publicity. However, history was to prove that early claims were over-optimistic.

Though they had the main advantage of cleanliness, electric cookers and hotplates still had too many teething troubles to seriously compete with gas. The elements were not reliable, they were slow, uncontrollable and too expensive to run, besides which the market had already been captured by robust cast-iron ranges and gas cookers which had been built to last. In a fit of early exuberance, the City of London Electric Lighting Company held a banquet on 15 June 1894 where the food was cooked by electricity. Like shrewd businessmen, they followed this up in July with an advertising leaflet offering electrical ovens on sale from £7/10/- to £14/14/- or for hire at 7/- to 12/- per quarter. Jumping on the band-wagon, in January 1895, all-electric cooking classes were offered by Miss Fairclough of the Gloucester Road School of Cooking, London. But all this seemed to have very little impact on the buying public, except that the feedback the hiring companies got from repairs and maintenance indicated areas for improvement.

The earliest cookers resembled safes (15), but the style soon settled down into a more or less straight copy of the gas cooker. The oven elements, which had originally been above and below the cooking area, were found to be more effective if placed to either side of it. They were usually made by bonding the heating element to the underside of a cast-iron plate using enamel, but these took a long time to heat up and cool down. For instance, it was recommended that an oven should be switched on for half an hour before it was required for use. To get the best results out of the boiling plates a heavy cast-iron pan had to be used, but these were clumsy and unpopular with the new self-sufficient housewife who preferred lighter aluminium ones. It took until 1926 for any real improvement to appear, which came in the guise of the metal-sheathed element from America. This could be bent during manufacture into whatever shape desired and so could serve the oven, grill or hotplate. Nevertheless, electric cookers scored several 'firsts' despite their poor showing when it came to sales.

As early as 1912 the Carron Iron Company produced a double-doored cooker (16), the oven lined with grey enamel sheets and the inner door made of glass. The control switches were large and cumbersome though, and so they were mounted on a wooden board fixed to the wall above the cooker. Each switch had its own fuse, and a light indicated which hotplates were on. But this impressive appliance had one glaring error; to reach the switches one had to lean across the hotplates and steaming saucepans and face the risk of getting burnt or electrocuted.

The first lightweight cooker was electric, and made in 1919 by

Belling (*17*). Their 'Modernette' was made of sheet steel instead of cast iron. The first split-level cooker was electric and was made early in the century (*19*). A Scottish professor who decided to build himself an all-electric house, purchased one and told the members of the Institution of Electrical Engineers in 1926 how much he liked it with its 'oven alongside the boiling table. This avoids stooping or kneeling when attending the oven—the low oven seems to be designed to cause irritation . . .' How right he was, but it seems to have taken many years before this simple fact was rediscovered in the 1960s. At a cost of over £30 the split-level cooker was not cheap, and with heating controls only capable of low, medium and high settings, this type of cooker was not drawing much trade away from the gas showrooms. The missing convenience was the thermostat, which was first applied to electric cookers in 1931 when the Creda cooker was fitted with the 'Credastat'. The cheap electric thermostat was the breakthrough which finally began to close the competition between gas and electricity. From the 1930s onwards sales were at last beginning to improve. By 1939 there were one and a half million electric cookers in Britain, compared with nine million gas cookers, proving what an uneconomical luxury they had been since their introduction in the 1890s.

Pots and pans

The eighteenth-century kitchen had rows of gleaming brass and copper saucepans which were heavy to use, impressive to look at and tedious to clean. In Victorian times they gradually gave way to cast iron which was no less heavy but at least it did not require so much polishing. Pan handles and lids were made of lighter tinplate, the handles being hollow so they would not transmit so much of the heat. But there were no holes in their ends by which they could be hung up, so in many kitchens pots and pans sat upside-down on a shelf with their lids hanging from nails below them.

There were special pans for every job: the fish kettle, a low oval dish with a lid for boiling or baking fish; the double boiler or bain marie for sauces requiring a controlled low heat; the multi-tiered steamer which cooked vegetables in steam, so retaining the taste and

9

goodness usually poured away in the boiling water; the salamander, which was not a pot but a piece of iron on the end of a long handle. It was put in the fire until glowing red hot and then held over food to brown it. It only fell into disuse when gas and electric cookers appeared with fitted grills; the pressure-cooker, the principle of which had been known since its invention by Denis Papin in the seventeenth century. A Frenchman working in London, Papin demonstrated a 'steam digester' in 1697. The nineteenth-century model (21) was made of cast iron with a conical weight acting as a safety-valve and worked at a pressure of about 3 lb per square inch before the steam would lift the valve. By 1930 cast aluminium models had pressure gauges on the top and were capable of withstanding up to 50 lb per square inch (20). The aluminium they were made of was first used in any quantity in the 1890s. A method of making aluminium was devised in 1844 but the process was very expensive and its use confined to treasures, such as a set of spoons commissioned by Emperor Napoleon III. Production remained minute—in 1880 America's total import amounted to no more than 500 lb! With the introduction of an electrolytic process in 1886, production rose dramatically and the price fell twentyfold. As the basic ore alumina is the third most abundant on the earth, the major cost was for electricity. To make one ton of aluminium in 1890 took 2 tons of ore and 20,000 kilowatt-hours of electricity. Early pots and pans were made of cast aluminium, but later they were pressed from sheets and called stamped aluminium ware.

The ultimate cooking pan was offered on sale in the early 1930s. It had a plug-in electric element and was called the Stokes 'Table Cooker'. The advertisements boasted that this electric frying-pan with its deep lid was also recommended for toasting, heating flat irons, boiling kettles, cooking food, warming plates or using as a radiator or fire—and all that for only 27/6d. in 1932.

Preserving food

Ice has been used to preserve food since Roman times but the major developments in refrigeration occurred in the nineteenth century in connection with transportation of fresh meat from places like South

America and Australia. Refrigeration in the domestic sense was a question of daily deliveries of fresh ice which was kept in a wooden ice box (27). It was lined in zinc or slate, with a wall of cork, ash, charcoal or even seaweed separating the inner lining from the wooden outer casing to provide a fairly effective insulation. By 1856 it had been realised that rather than simply laying food on the ice, the cooling characteristics improved if ice was put in an upper compartment and air allowed to circulate round it (25), keeping the food in the lower compartment cool.

Commercial cooling had been applied to various industries such as brewing and candle-making in the 1850s, but as they used a steam engine to pump the refrigerant, they were too large and noisy for domestic use. However, a demand was clearly there and it was not long before it was exploited. The New York annual consumption of ice by 1882 was as high as 1,450 lb per head, much of this being used by factories and shops, some for cooling air in theatres (the Madison Square Theatre consumed 4 tons of ice put into the air stream each evening) and the rest for home use, cooling drinks, preserving food or making ice-cream.

Some ice boxes had a tap on the side for obtaining cold water from the melting ice (26), but as there was a chance of this being impure and contaminated, it was passed through a filter before drinking. Water filters worked on various principles, but the most common was a double ceramic vessel (33). The outer vessel was of glazed stoneware and therefore impervious to water, while the inner one was of a porous ceramic known as biscuit-ware. This allowed the water to trickle slowly through to the outer container from where it could be tapped off at will. All the impurities were absorbed by a filter, usually of silicated carbon, which would be replaced at intervals. A salt-glazed stoneware model of this type of 2½ gallons capacity sold in London for a guinea in 1904. Other models fitted straight on to the cold-water tap (34) so that all the water was filtered. These used a bed of charcoal through which the water was forced by the pressure of the mains. The market was served by many manu-facturers, though few can have had so many variations as Berkfield's, who offered both types already described, as well as table models (capacity $2\frac{1}{2}$ pints), travelling models and field models with their own pumps.

The first American patent for an ice-cream freezer was taken out in 1848. A smaller household model followed the commercial machine and became very popular in the 1880s (29). It consisted of two buckets, one inside the other, the centre one for cream, and the surrounding space for a mixture of ice and salt. There was a crank handle on top which rotated a paddle in the inner bucket and mixed the cream as it froze. This kept the ice crystals small. Fresh fruit or juice could be added, some machines having the centre compartment divided down the middle for making two different flavours at the same time. The Cincinnati Gooch Freezer Company ran an advertisement in 1889 for their whole range of machines which boasted: 'The PEERLESS are the best. But they are a little higher priced than others, but are well worth the difference. The ZERO is cheaper, not so good as the Peerless, but better than any other Freezer on the market. The PET, cheaper than the Zero, and a very good one. The BOSS are very low priced. Anybody could afford to buy one. All are good, solid and well made', and Gooches were only one of hundreds of such companies all over Europe and America.

The domestic refrigerator could have become a reality after Tesla's electric motor was first marketed by Westinghouse Inc. in 1888, but it wasn't until 1913 that the Domelre (*Domestic Electric Refrigerator*) was on sale in Chicago as the first household machine. In 1914, the Detroit firm of Kelvinator used an electric motor to replace the steam engine which had worked the compressor. Because by this time the refrigerant used had changed from ammonia to sulphur dioxide, it was recommended that their $\frac{1}{8}$ horsepower motor and compressor should be housed in the cellar and linked to an existing ice box in the kitchen by a pipe. If anything leaked the room would have been filled with a 'bad-egg' smell, so the further away the power unit could be, the better. Their first self-contained household refrigerator took a further eleven years to perfect and in 1925 both the 'Kelvinette' and the Electrolux gas refrigerator appeared. As the cooling unit was rather bulky on the early models some manufacturers like BTH of Rugby located it on top outside the food compartment (*28*). It did include an ice-making compartment, but this was really nothing new, as the 'Champion' hand ice-making machine (*24*) had been on sale as much as thirty-five years earlier.

Refrigerators allowed the cook to preserve her own food for short periods, but she was still bound by seasonal produce, gluts and shortages in the market, unless she stocked her larder with tinned foods. As early as 1795 Napoleon had offered a prize of 12,000 francs to anyone who could improve provisions for his armies. A Frenchman, François Appert, won the prize by originating the process of cooking food and sealing it in glass bottles. In England in 1810 Peter Durrand patented the process of using tinplate canisters or 'cans' which made a lighter container, an important feature when their products were designed specifically for the forces who would be carrying their supplies with them. By 1812 his patent had been taken up and the first cannery in Bermondsey, London, supplied soups and preserved meats to the Navy who were involved in the American War.

Unfortunately the process was largely misunderstood and the food was often bad. The mistake had been in using cans that were too large, which meant the food in the centre was not always properly sterilised. Smaller cans were found to be the answer and by 1847 considerable quantities of canned meat were exported from Australia. Louis Pasteur's work on bacteria in 1860 clarified the scientific principles involved and from then on efficient canning became widespread. In this day of tomato soup and baked beans it is seldom realised that even after its uncertain beginnings, tinned food has been a reality for well over a hundred years. Stretching a point it could be said that in a roundabout way Napoleon is responsible for the empty tins that litter our modern society!

The question remained—how did you open the can? Having devised a method of filling them, this aspect was somewhat ignored. As late as 1840 tins were still sold with the following directions printed on them: 'cut round the top near to the outer edge with a chisel and a hammer'! The first domestic can-opener dates from the 1860s and was sold along with the stocks of bully beef. To identify it from any subsequent rivals, the handle had a cast-iron bull's head and a long tail (*30*). It had a two-ended blade, one fashioned into a sharp point for piercing the tin, and the other with a cutting edge for inserting into the hole and see-sawing around the rim. This type of opener was widely produced for over sixty years, though was not sold in England until the mid-1880s.

Commodities like baked beans were first canned in 1875 for sale to American fishing crews who could not be home for the traditional 'beanfeast' that was part of the Saturday night meal, though the familiar tomato sauce recipe was not made until 1880. Heinz, whose trade-mark was the pickled cucumber, first introduced baked beans into Britain in 1905.

Food preparation

Preparing food for a large household kept the kitchen staff busy all day. It is not surprising that with all the time-consuming activities any rationalisation or mechanisation was welcomed by the domestics.

The act of cutting things up received a lot of attention including improvements to knives themselves and also gadgets to do tedious repetitive operations. Knives were made of ordinary steel until stainless steel was introduced in the 1920s. Until then they were hand forged and prone to rusting. They were sharpened on long steels usually by the carver at table, but for those whose main worry was serving a portion of finger along with the meat, there were alternative patent sharpeners (35). The professional carver poured scorn on these gadgets while flashing his blade through the air, but they were the perfect face-saver for anyone else. The knife was simply drawn backwards across a 'V' of hardened steel pieces. Some versions were even made so the angle of the 'V' could be adjusted.

Borrowing an idea from the carpenter's saw, a serrated knife, on the other hand, did not require constant resharpening. The Christy Bread Knife Company of London made their almost handle-less model in the early 1890s (36).

If knives weren't kept clean and dry they would rust, so treating them as part of the washing-up was asking for trouble. However, if the kitchen could boast a Rotary Knife Cleaner (37), the story was one of bliss—except for the poor servant who had to work the machine. After scrubbing them clean, the knives were inserted into holes around its rim (Kent's patent knife-cleaner of 1882 took four knives, other models took six) and a special abrasive powder, such as Oakey's 'Britannia Knife Polish' was poured into one of the holes. The knives would be subjected to a vigorous cleaning and polishing when the large crank handle was turned. Alternate felt pads and bristles were pushed past both sides of each knife and a couple of dozen turns would make them bright and beautiful. The machines, like the 'Uneek' knife-cleaner of 1890 (*38*), began to disappear in the 1930s due to the increasing use of stainless-steel cutlery. Of course the silver fruit knives never saw the cruel insides of the Rotary Knife Cleaner, and they gave the footman hours of endless toil cleaning them before the butler locked them all away each night in the walk-in safe with the rest of the household silver.

The more simple chopping jobs were done with purpose-built gadgets such as the sugar nipper, a sort of clumsy scissors for cutting loaf-sugar, which was sold in cones up to 3 ft long and weighing about 14 lb. Others got more ambitious and included gears and flywheels to make the job easier, though it often took longer to set the machine up than do the job by hand! With no electricity, power was provided by muscles, but that is why there were servants. One mid-nineteenth-century food chopper and mixer paid its homage to the giant beam engine. On a much-reduced scale this little machine looked like a copy of the steam pumping engines used in deep mines, but instead of driving pumps to raise water from the drowned workings, it moved a little knife blade rapidly up and down inside a slowly revolving container. To remove the bowl you had to uncouple the beam from the crank handle and raise the blades clear. Either that or tip the whole thing upside down . . .

In 1880 the Danes made a bread slicer (*31*) that had the annoying habit of crushing the loaf to a concertina shape before actually passing through it (though the French still use this type of machine, known as the guillotine, for chopping those long loaves up, which being mainly crust, survive admirably). Where the look of the end product was not so important, the bread slicer was ideal—not much use for wafer-thin cucumber sandwiches though.

By the 1890s manufacturers excelled themselves in modifications

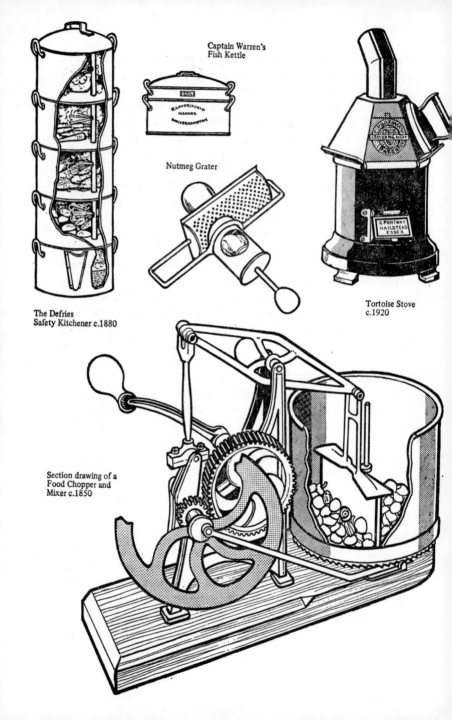

Captain Warren's
Fish Kettle

Nutmeg Grater

The Defries
Safety Kitchener c.1880

Tortoise Stove
c.1920

Section drawing of a
Food Chopper and
Mixer c.1850

to basic cutting machines. The Spong Company produced a bean slicer which accepted french beans, one by one, fed through a hole in the side and on to a rotary knife. With three blades on it, a bean soon appeared as a pile of fine slices on a plate below. Spongs took the precaution of providing two holes to feed the beans in, one for large beans and the other for small. That allowed the French to pick their vegetables young and tender, and the English to grow them into stringy giants; *chacun à son goût*!

One of the more fascinating machines was the apple peeler which first appeared as a jumble of painted cast-iron cog teeth as early as 1863 (*39*). It had to perform two functions; the first one, to revolve the apple on a spindle and the second to move a cutting knife in an arc which matched the profile of the apple. The knife was held against the apple using a spring and a handle was turned which revolved the fruit and so removed the peel in a single strip. Designed for hard cooking apples, there was usually enough resistance in the fruit to keep the blade from sinking in too far. However, bruised or soft fruit was beyond this gadget as the blade would disappear into a fleshy part and then dislodge the apple from its spindle. Because of this basic limitation, it became obvious this type of machine was also suitable for peeling potatoes. Goodell's White Mountain Potato Parer (*32*) was one such American model on sale *c*. 1875 for $1. The same firm continued in the 'peeling' market and went on to make more sophisticated machines such as the Dandy apple peeler which was produced in 1898. This caterer's model not only peeled the apple, cored it and cut it into an attractive spiral, but also ejected the finished fruit and pushed the core off too. It was a maze of intricate cogs and levers, a large cumbersome machine, which once in motion was a joy to watch. A couple of turns of the handle took the machine through its complete cycle—the slow part was getting it to the 'start' position and fixing the apple securely on the prong.

Spong's hand-operated mincer (*45*) has hardly changed since its introduction except that some lightening was possible with the introduction of cast aluminium in the late 1880s, and yet its sister, the sausage-making machine (*43*), has entirely disappeared. It was patented in 1862 by Hales and used the slow screw thread as the forcing device in the same way as the mincer does, but instead of pushing the content through a rotating cutter, it pushed it out through a nozzle into a gut casing which had to be clamped on to it. The forcing action also appeared in the lemon squeezer—not the shaped glass mound with a tray around the bottom, where you twist the fruit by hand, but a lever-operated version which gave you greater pressure (50). Thornhill's produced their model in 1887.

In 1895 the Enterprise Manufacturing Company of Philadelphia marketed a raisin stoner (41) which removed the flesh from the stones, but it produced somewhat shredded raisins as the result. The raisins first had to be soaked, and were then pulled through two toothed rollers which tore off the flesh. This fell through the bottom of the machine, while the stones stayed above. By reversing the handle the stones were released and the rollers cleared, but the whole process was slow and messy.

For stoning the occasional cherry there was a hand-held device which forced a rod through the fruit, pushing the stone out of the other side. The mechanical cherry stoner was a more sophisticated machine for larger quantities which removed the stones without severely damaging the fruit. It was able to rely on the assumption that cherries were similar in shape and size and the stone was in the middle, unlike the raisin stoner. The machine was also cleverer in its action because it pushed the stones out of one hole and the cherries out of another, allowing each to be caught in different bowls.

Besides chopping, food preparation involved weighing (53,54), mixing, blending and beating, and to this day the basic mixer is still the revolving egg-beater type. Patented in 1873, the 'egg-beater' is essentially the hand-operated machine we still use, but it was then made of a mixture of cast iron and pressed iron sheet with tinned blades. Minor variations appeared all over its native America, heavier models for clamping to the table, others built inside mixing bowls, and by 1918 even electrically driven.

This is the first time we have met the use of the small electric motor but it has proved to be the key invention in the history of domestic gadgets. Thomas Edison made a very small electric motor as early as 1880, but since the introduction of the commercial motor in

1888 which was a bulky and heavy unit of about 2 feet cube, it took a further thirty years before the electric motor could be mass produced small enough to be of any use in the home. Large appliances such as washing-machines were able to benefit earlier from this new source of power, but even the $\frac{1}{8}$th horsepower motor which they used was still about 5 inches diameter and nearly a foot long—hardly the model to build into the handle of an egg whisk. Nevertheless, there had been a demand for a stirring apparatus for use in chemistry laboratories and by 1904 an electric mixer was on sale in London whose motor was not larger than 3 inches in any one direction. It could provide the obvious power source for small gadgets and so it was not surprising that the earliest domestic electric mixer was an almost straight copy. In fact the 'Universal' mixer-beater (40) by Landers, Frary and Clark of Connecticut was simply the identical laboratory motor strapped on to a hand-driven egg whisk, no attempt having been made to build it into the appliance. This early model had fixed beaters, but rival manufacturers were soon offering alternative attachments which by 1930 included dough mixers, lemon squeezers, mincers, flour sifters, cheese graters and knife sharpeners, all for the same machine.

Flavouring food was done in the same way as today, home grown and dried herbs being added according to what was being cooked. However, they were not kept in rows of glass bottles, a convention stolen from the apothecaries shop, but in herb boxes. These were round containers with a domed lid and a ring on the top, but inside there were several small walls, dividing the space up like slices of cake. Each compartment held a different herb or spice and the centre hole contained whole nutmegs and a special cylindrical grater. Opening the box released a variety of evocative fragrances. The small grater was reserved solely for nutmeg, any other job having its own grater of a different size (46)—for lemon, for Parmesan cheese, for Cheddar, for slicing cucumber and so on.

Hot water

Washing-up for a house full of people has always been an awful chore because it never seems to end. It is interesting to note that the first practical dishwashing machine was invented by a woman in 1889. With the old problem of having to heat endless kettles on the hob, back-boilers and geysers had gone a long way to ease the burden. From the late 1890s multi-point geysers such as Ewart's 'Califont' supplied hot water to a number of taps, so the kitchen had its own supply and the hard work of carrying pitchers of hot water to hand basins around the house was avoided.

In the kitchen, soap was shaved from large cakes, all the left-over ends being kept in a wire basket on the end of a handle, which could be swished around in the water to strengthen the lather. Household soap emerged in the 1840s as a by-product of the alkali industry, whose main products were bleaching powder for the textile industry and soda for glass works, but only became cheap when Gladstone repealed the soap tax in 1853. The consumption in Britain rose from 90,000 tons in 1850 to 300,000 tons in 1900. Brands such as 'Gossage's Dry Soap', Lever Brothers 'Sunlight' and Hedley's 'Fairy' filled the shops, while the chemical factories that produced them filled the sky with dense black smoke. The answer to all this pollution was to build very tall chimneys which released the smoke higher up and allowed it to be carried further away so it descended over some other area—like the next town!

Despite a patent of 1865 for a commercial machine, it was not until 1899 that the American housewife was offered a solution to her washing-up problems in the shape of the domestic dishwasher, invented by a Mrs Cockran of Indiana. (The European market for such a machine was virtually non-existent until the late 1950s.) It was a wooden tub which was wheeled over to the sink and filled first with the dirty dishes and then hot water from a bucket. Then a handle was cranked to provide power to a set of air plungers which drove water over the dishes. Mercifully the machine was fitted with an electric motor in 1914 to become the first automatic dishwasher. 'Automatic' meant the motor drove the washers. The machine still had to be filled with water by hand, and afterwards drained back into the bucket from a stopcock at the bottom.

Heating large quantities of water was usually done by solid fuel or gas geyser, but for smaller amounts, the electric kettle (22) had a lot to offer. Well, once it had got over its early problems, that is. The idea of using electricity for heating food was first patented in 1879 and led to the slow development of cookers. At the same time the heating elements were fixed to all kinds of appliances from frying-pans to foot-warmers, wall radiators to kettles. An 1897 catalogue of Crompton and Co., Chelmsford, offered a 3-pint kettle for £1/15/– and proudly claimed 'The 3-Pint Kettle will Boil Cold Water in from 15 to 20 minutes', which was hardly a great threat to the gas stove boiling-ring which did the same job in 5 minutes! The snag was that the electric kettle had its heating element built into the thickness of the base, and should it break, could not be repaired. The situation improved when screw-on elements were developed in 1911, which could be fixed to the bottom of existing kettles that were previously non-electric or interchanged by the dealer if they required repairing. And there was the clue as to why the boiling period was so long—being fixed externally to the bottom of a kettle, half the heat was wasted downwards! It was not until a patent in 1922 by A. L. Large that the heating element was set in a tube and totally immersed in the water. The first kettle on the market using this improvement was the 'Swan' kettle by Bulpitt and Sons of Birmingham, and incidentally pioneered the use of the tubular element that was to be adapted for cookers in 1926. (The difference was that the kettle used wire wound round flat mica and inserted into a flat copper tube, while the cooker element had the wire supported in a bed of magnesium oxide.)

A variety of safety devices were developed ranging from a plug that melted on overheating thus breaking the contact (Landers, Frary and Clark 1916), to a spring-loaded device which ejected the plug if the element overheated (A. L. Large 1926), and a resettable self-ejecting safety plug (H. W. Bulpitt 1931). Most early electric cookers on hire included a free 3-pint electric kettle. At first the electricity generating companies charged a fixed sum for power used for lighting as against power used for cooking which was on the 'units consumed' system, until they discovered many housewives were plugging their kettles into the light socket and so getting their hot water for nothing.

Washing machines

Hot water was also used for washing clothes, though for a long time gadgets that were intended to make the job easier required almost as much effort to work them as the traditional washboards, scrubbing-brush and peggy had done. The washing machine first appeared in the 1850s in the form of a wooden tub with a dolly set vertically in the lid. The dolly or peggy looked like a milking stool on the end of a stick and had originally been twisted backwards and forwards by hand. Now this motion was done automatically by turning a handle, but like the later dishwasher, the tub still had to be filled and emptied by hand. In about 1914 electric motors were added to the familiar hand-operated machines, and the dolly driven through a short belt drive. The motors were seldom earthed and because they were usually fixed to the underside of the machine, the likelihood of water dripping through a leaky tub on to the motor below was extremely high. The similarity between the hand-operated and motor-operated machine suggests that the alternative power unit was first conceived as an optional extra depending on the size of your purse or the strength of your laundrymaid's arm. The arrival of the electric motor did not automatically mean all washing machines were power-driven from then on. Hand-operated models continued to be widespread for the next thirty years, some using a paddle rotated backwards and forwards, and others relying on a more basic method of agitating the clothes. The 'Faithfull' cradle washing machine (55) had its ancestors mixed in butter-churn and rocking-horse stables. Its legs could be stowed away, allowing the hollow elongated tub to be rocked backwards and forwards. Clothes were fed in through a removable hatch at the top, likewise water and grated soap. If only the inventor had fitted a saddle on top, the weekly work could have become a useful part of a child's toy, but as it was it remained in the realm of the servant's drudgery.

There was rarely any method of heating the water once it was in the washing machine, though there were exceptions such as the gas-heated models sold by Morton's in the 1880s. Their Patent Steam Washer (61) came on a metal stand which had a built-in gas burner.

1. Cambrian Kitchen Range by Carron c.1890

2. 'Larbert' Cottage Range
   c.1895

3. Solid Fuel Stove. 1890

4. Aga Cooker 1929

5. Sears & Roebuck
   Solid Fuel Kitchener 1899

6. Albion 'Sunrise' Paraffin Stove
   c.1910

7. 'Albionette' Dinner Stove

8. The Defries
   Safety Kitchener c.1880

9. Paraffin Stove 1882

10. Argand Base-burner
    Oil Stove c.1875

11. Wooden Gas Stove
    c.1850

12. Universal Gas Cooker
    by R.A.Main c.1866

13. Sugg's Gas Cooker
    c.1886

14. A Gas Ring

16. 'Carron' Electric Cooker c.1912

15. GEC Electric Cooker
Archer System   1895

17. Belling 'Modernette'
1919

18. GEC Electric Cooker
with double glass door
1927

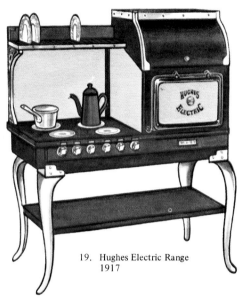

19. Hughes Electric Range
1917

20. L'Auto Thermus
Pressure Cooker 1930

21. Digestor Pressure Cooker
c.1860

22. Swan Electric Kettle
1921

23. Electric Frying Pan
1898

24. 'Champion'
Ice-making machine
1890

THE CHAMPION

26. Ice Chest c.1907

ELLIS'S PATENT

ICE CHAMBER

THE SNOWDON
MADE IN ENGLAND
REFRIGERATOR

25. 'Alaska' Refrigerator
c.1870

27. Seeger Refrigerator c.1890

28. General Electric c.1927

29. White Mountain Freezer for ice cream 1923

30. CAN-OPENERS

'Kutout' c.1930

'Blue Streak' c.1930

Bull's Head
c.1885

Bull's Head
c.1890

Spike and Cutter
1902

31. Raadvad Bread Slicer
c.1880

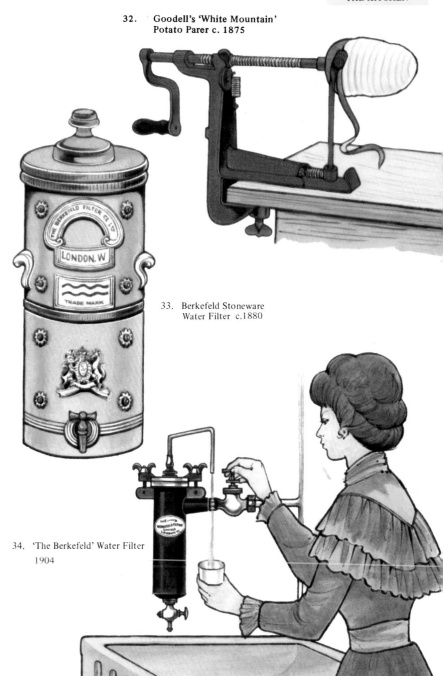

32. Goodell's 'White Mountain'
Potato Parer c. 1875

33. Berkefeld Stoneware
Water Filter c.1880

34. 'The Berkefeld' Water Filter
1904

35. 'Benstill' Knife Sharpe

36. Christy Bread Knife 18

THE WONDERFUL CHRISTY BREAD KNIFE
Regᵈ 195404
UNDER ROYAL LETTERS PATENT

37. Kent's Patent Rotary Disc Knife Cleaner 1882

38. 'Uneek' Knife Cleaner c.1890

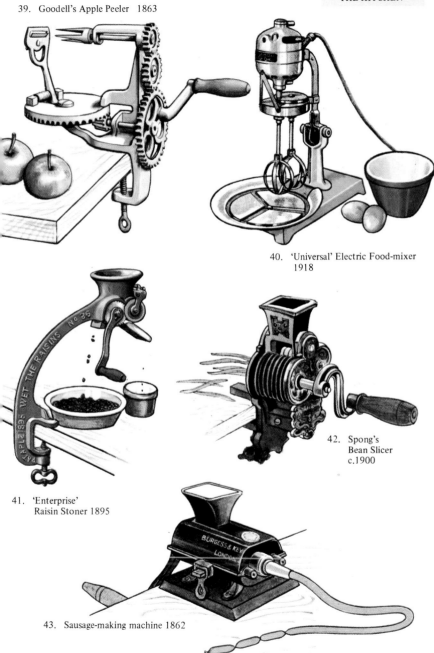

39. Goodell's Apple Peeler 1863

40. 'Universal' Electric Food-mixer 1918

41. 'Enterprise' Raisin Stoner 1895

42. Spong's Bean Slicer c.1900

43. Sausage-making machine 1862

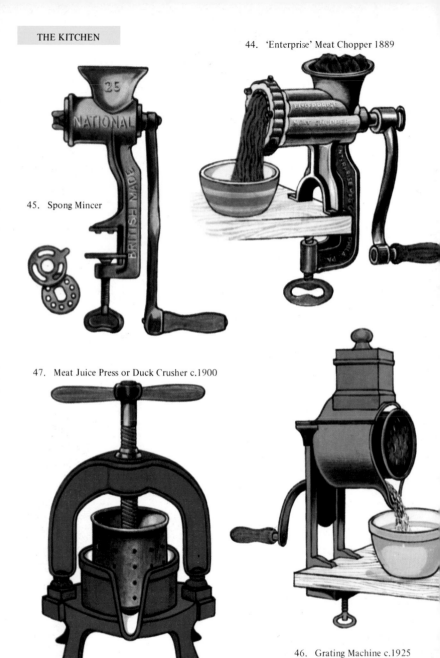

44. 'Enterprise' Meat Chopper 1889

45. Spong Mincer

47. Meat Juice Press or Duck Crusher c.1900

46. Grating Machine c.1925

48. Coffee Mill 1840

'The Rapid' Lemon Squeezer

49. Quick Grinding Coffee Mill

51. 'Kleenquick' Boot Cleaning Appliance 1890

2. Revolving Boot and Shoe Cleaner c.1905

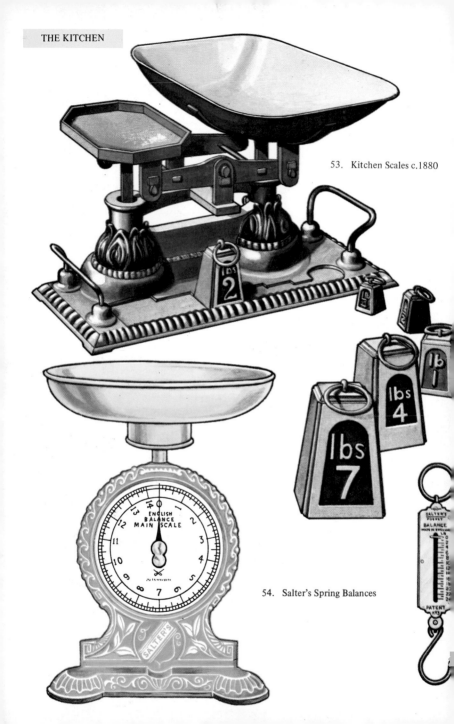

53. Kitchen Scales c.1880

54. Salter's Spring Balances

55. 'Faithfull' Cradle Washing Machine 1906

56. Ewbank 'Queen' Mangle c.1907

57. Bradford 'Vowell Y' Washing Machine 1897

58. Sellers Washing Machine and Mangle c.1850

59. Krauss Coal-fired Washing Machine Electrically driven 1923

60. Red Star Mangle c.1914

61. Morton's Steam Washing Machine 1884

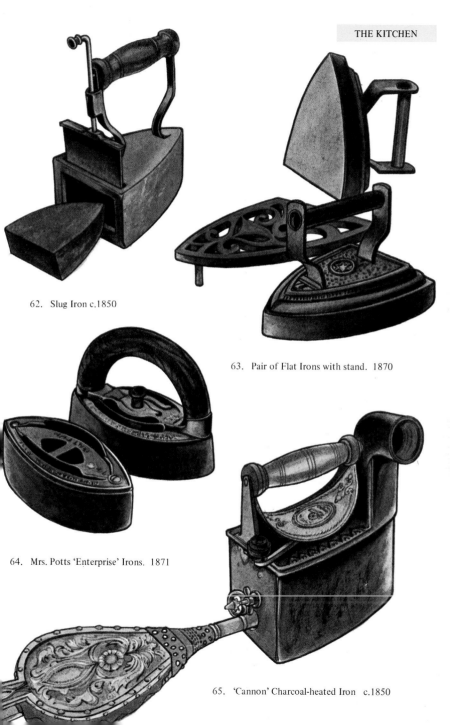

62. Slug Iron c.1850

63. Pair of Flat Irons with stand. 1870

64. Mrs. Potts 'Enterprise' Irons. 1871

65. 'Cannon' Charcoal-heated Iron c.1850

66. Carbon Arc Iron c.1880

67. 'Prometheus' Electric Iron. 1

68. Electric Iron 1898

69. The 'Eastlake' Clothes Stick 1879

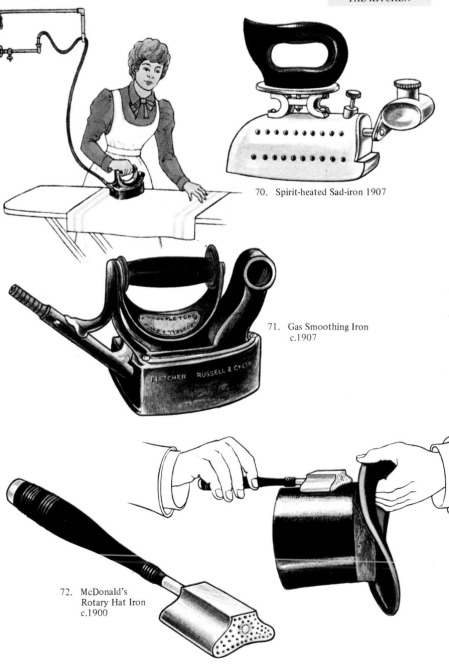

70. Spirit-heated Sad-iron 1907

71. Gas Smoothing Iron c.1907

72. McDonald's Rotary Hat Iron c.1900

73. Booth's Original
    Street Vacuum Cleaner 1901

74. Trolle[y]
    Vacu[um]
    Clean[er]
    1906

75. Bissell's
    'Grand Rapids'
    Carpet Sweeper 1876

76. Griffith Foot-operated Cleaner 1905

77. The 'Wizard' Cleaner 1912

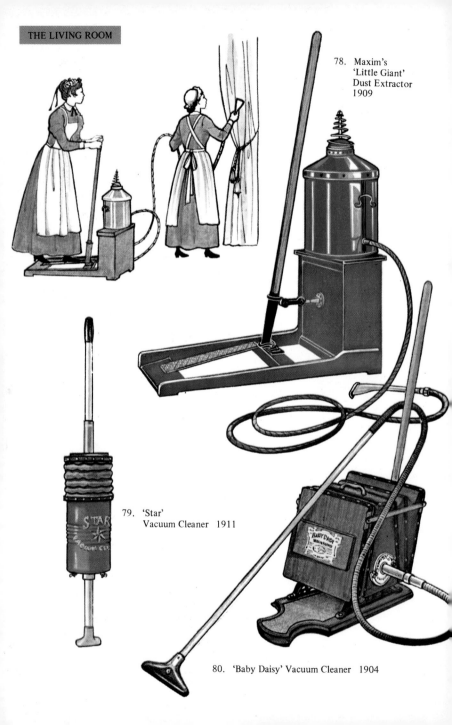

78. Maxim's 'Little Giant' Dust Extractor 1909

79. 'Star' Vacuum Cleaner 1911

80. 'Baby Daisy' Vacuum Cleaner 1904

81. 'The Air Way' 1930

82. Spangler's Vacuum Cleaner 1908

83. Hoover 1924

84. The Magic
Vacuum Cleaner 1915

85. 'Queen' Clockwork
    Fire-lighting Fan
    1898

86. Junkers & Ruh
    Solid Fuel Stove 1880

87. 'Little Gripper' Tongs c.1907

88. 'The Egg' Stove c.1914

89. 'The Sigma'
    Stove c.1910

90. Paraffin Stove c.1898

91. The 'Ardent'
Portable Table Heater
1890

92. Aluminium Paraffin Stove
1899

93. 'Lily' Paraffin Stove
1890

94. The 'Albion'
Paraffin Heater c.1895

95. Rippingille's
Paraffin Stoves c.1890

96. Gas Fire with
    Patent Ball Fuel Radiants c.1905

97. Gas Fire with
    Tufted Asbestos Radiants c.1882

98. 'Eagle' Gas Stove c.1870

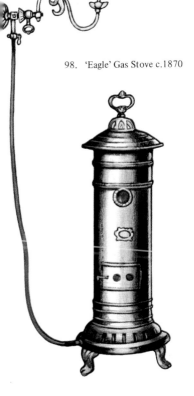

99. Carron Gas Fire 1910

100. Lawson Portable
Odourless Room Heater c.1910

101. Welsbach Kern
Portable Gas Fire c.18

102. Clark's Hygienic
Syphon Stove 1881

103. Omega Gas
Fire 1900

04. Carron Dowsing Bulb Fire c.1904

105. Crompton Panel Radiator 1897

106. Bastian 'Quartzalite' Fire 1909

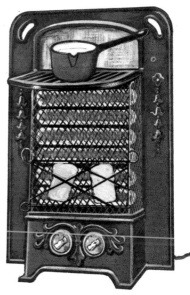

108. Belling 'Standard' 1913

'. 'Magnet' Portable Fire 1925

109. Radiator with oven 1911

110. 'Ideal' Domestic Boiler 1911

111. Belling Imitation Coal Fire 1921

112. Belling Electric
Convector Heater 1920

Oil Lamps

113. Sliding Suspension Lamp
c.1893

114. Hooded Piano Lamp
1907

115. Pillar Lamp

116. Bracket Lamp

117. Student Lamp
c.1840

Gas Lights

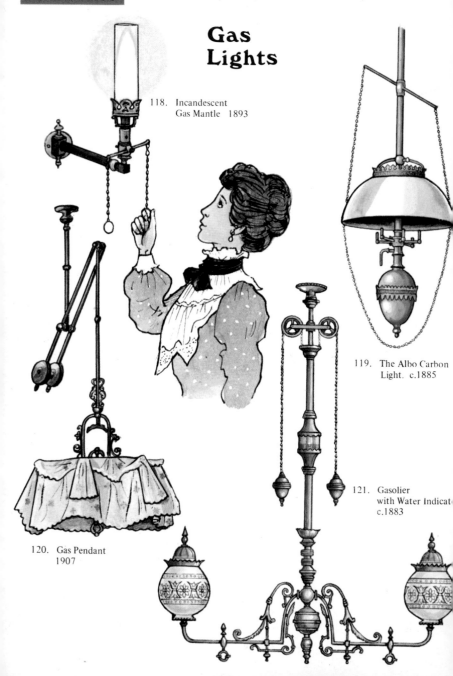

118. Incandescent Gas Mantle 1893

119. The Albo Carbon Light. c.1885

121. Gasolier with Water Indicat c.1883

120. Gas Pendant 1907

Electric Lights

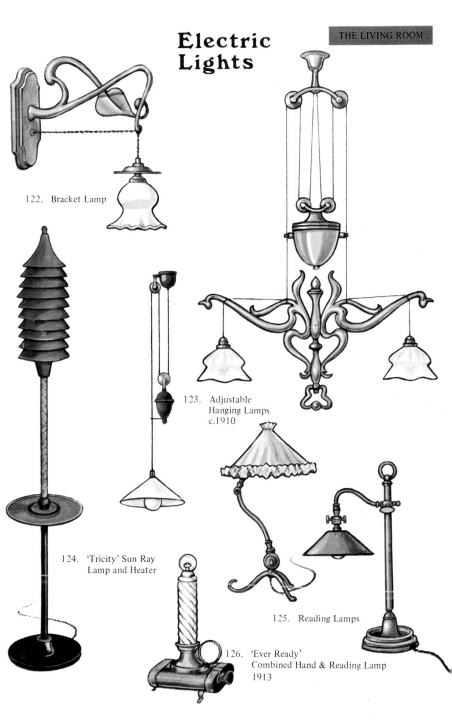

122. Bracket Lamp

123. Adjustable
       Hanging Lamps
       c.1910

124. 'Tricity' Sun Ray
       Lamp and Heater

125. Reading Lamps

126. 'Ever Ready'
       Combined Hand & Reading Lamp
       1913

127. Carter's Reclining
Invalid Chair and
'Carbrek' Bed-table
1910

128. Holloway Book-rest
and Dictionary Holder

129. Linenized Music Roll

MODERATO

LINENIZED MUSIC ROLLS

130. Autopiano 1909

131. Music Roll Storage Cabinet

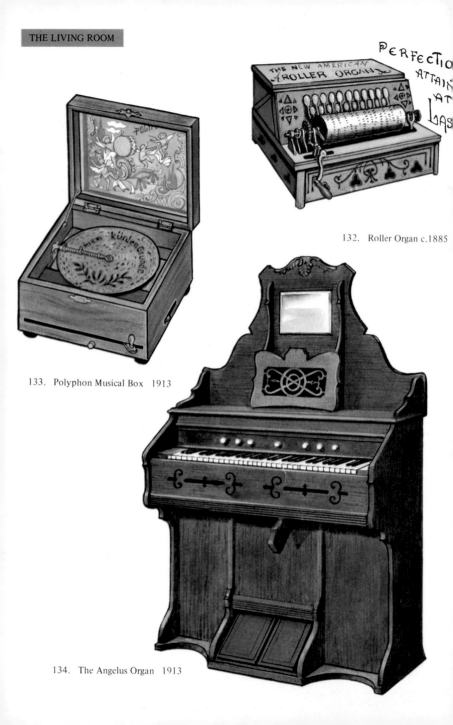

132.   Roller Organ c.1885

133.   Polyphon Musical Box   1913

134.   The Angelus Organ   1913

Phonographs

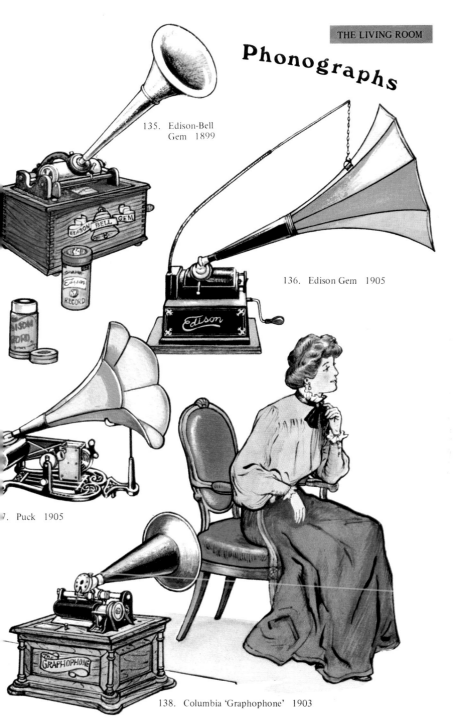

135. Edison-Bell Gem 1899

136. Edison Gem 1905

7. Puck 1905

138. Columbia 'Graphophone' 1903

Gramophones

139. Hand-driven Models 1898

140. Columbia
Graphophone
c.1902

141. HMV (Model No.5) 1898

142. Parlaphone 1912

143. Marconiphone V-2 Radio Receiver
1922

144. "Gecophone" Crystal Radio Receiver
1924

145. Themiodyne TF6 c.1924

146. Lumophon 5 Consolette 1932

147. De Forest Radio 1924

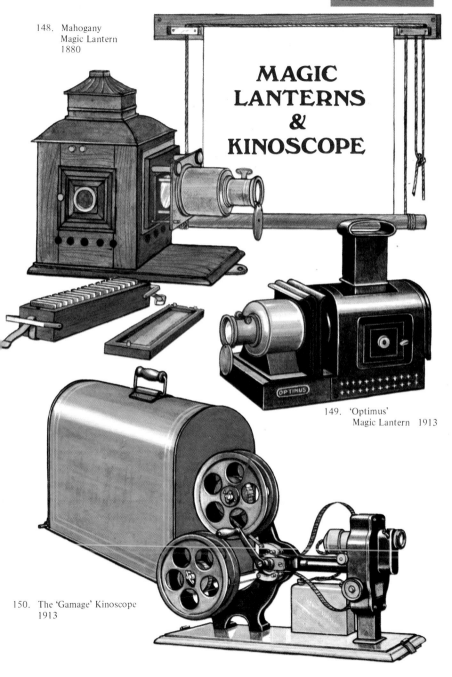

148. Mahogany Magic Lantern 1880

MAGIC LANTERNS & KINOSCOPE

149. 'Optimus' Magic Lantern 1913

150. The 'Gamage' Kinoscope 1913

152. Kinetoscope c.1895

THE VIVISCOPE
A KINETOSCOPIC TOY

MOVING FIGURES IN LIFE LIKE ACTION

A PERPETUAL THEATRE OF ENTERTAINMENT

151. The Holmes' Hand Stereoscope c.1885

153. Praxinoscope Theatre 1880

154. Brush Pen-wiper in holder

155. Ball-point Nib in Anti-blotting Holder

156. Automatic Pencil

157. Self-pointing Pencil

158. Multi-colour Pencil c.1907

159. Fountain-pen c.1900

160. Rocker Blotter, Calendar and Stamp Case

161. Stapler c.1907

162. Blickensderfer Typewriter 1907

163. The 'Merritt' Typewriter 1890

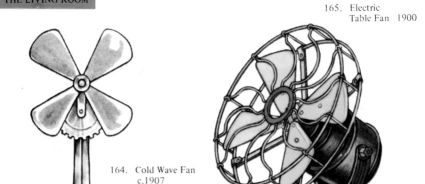

165. Electric
Table Fan 1900

164. Cold Wave Fan
c.1907

166. Battery Table Fan c.1910

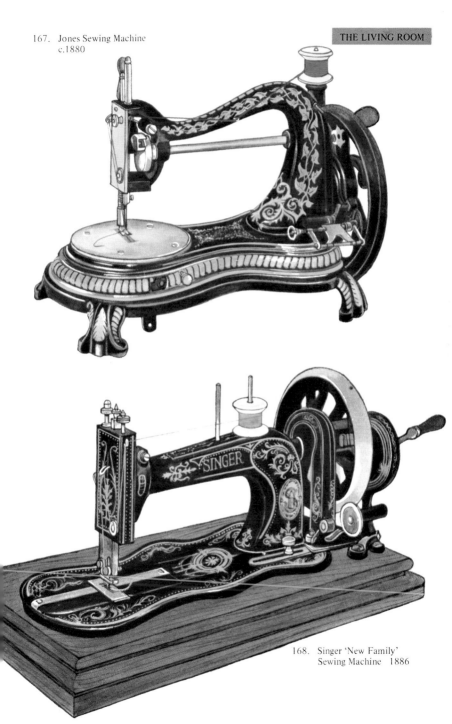

167. Jones Sewing Machine
     c.1880

168. Singer 'New Family'
     Sewing Machine 1886

169. The Royal Anchor
    Sewing Machine 1871

170. Singer Treadle
    Sewing Machin
    c.1880

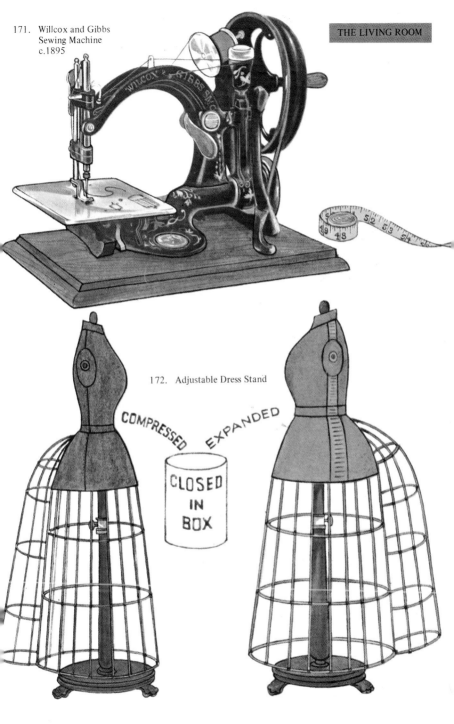

171. Willcox and Gibbs
Sewing Machine
c.1895

172. Adjustable Dress Stand

COMPRESSED EXPANDED

CLOSED
IN
BOX

c.1900

173. Egg Toppers

c.1887

174. Self-pouring Teapot
1888

175. Toast Crisper
c.1905

176. Detachable
Moustache Guard c.1895

177. 'Caffeta' Coffee Maker
c.1910

). 'Napierian'
Coffee Machine c.1907

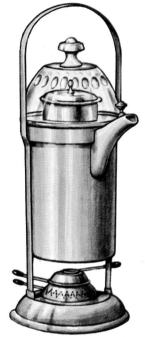

178. Coffee Percolator c.1902

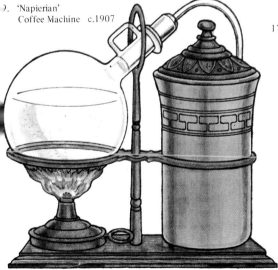

180. Corkscrews

181. Seltzogene 'Clincher' Soda Water Syphon c.1890

182. Sparklet Soda Water Syphon c.1910

183. Thornhill's Lemon Squeezer 1887

184. Brass Kettle with
Spirit Lamp and Stand
c.1913

185. 'Universal'
Electric Toaster
1913

186. Automatic Crystal Fountain
c.1870

187. Lemon
Squeezer 1909

The Delight
of Bathing

188. Foot's Safety First
Folding Bath Cabinet   c.1907

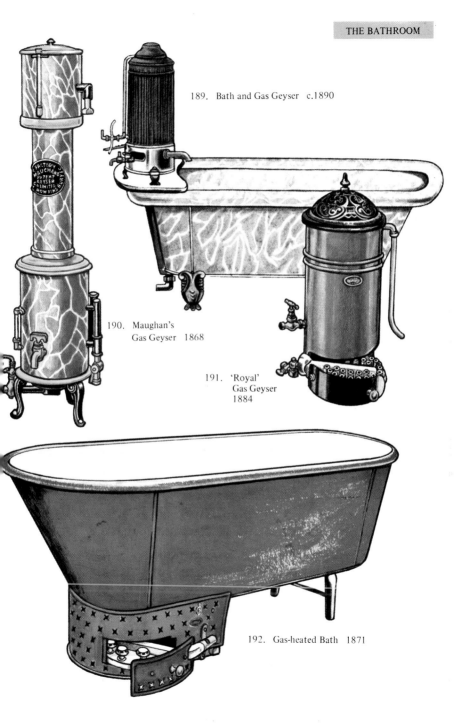

189. Bath and Gas Geyser c.1890

190. Maughan's Gas Geyser 1868

191. 'Royal' Gas Geyser 1884

192. Gas-heated Bath 1871

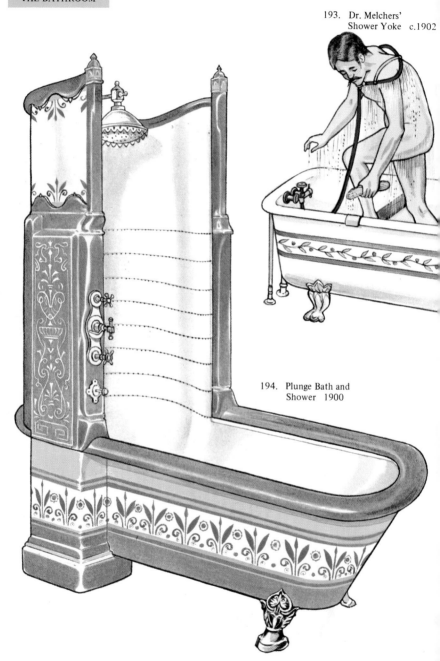

193. Dr. Melchers'
Shower Yoke c.1902

194. Plunge Bath and
Shower 1900

195. Kennedy Needle Shower
1916

FLOATS

IT IVORY

PEARS

196. Adamsez
Bath and Shower
c.1900

197. Kampfe Safety Razor and 'Diagonal' Strop c.1903

198. 'The Shavers' Friend' c.1898

199. Gillette Safety Razor 1904

200. 'Valet' Autostrop Razor

201. Electric Shaving Pot c.1898

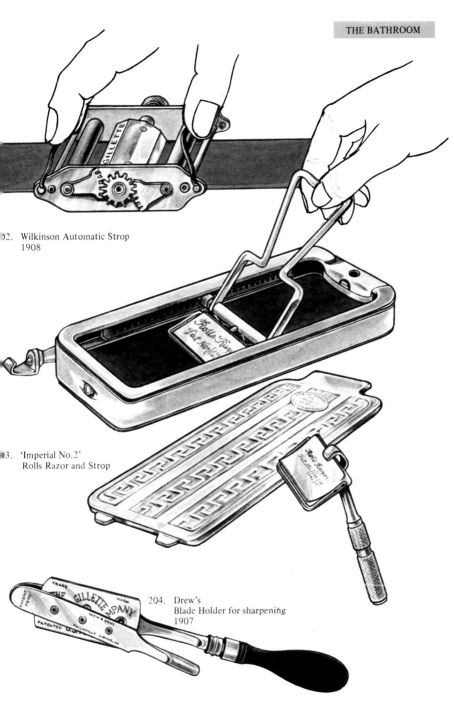

202. Wilkinson Automatic Strop
1908

203. 'Imperial No.2'
Rolls Razor and Strop

204. Drew's
Blade Holder for sharpening
1907

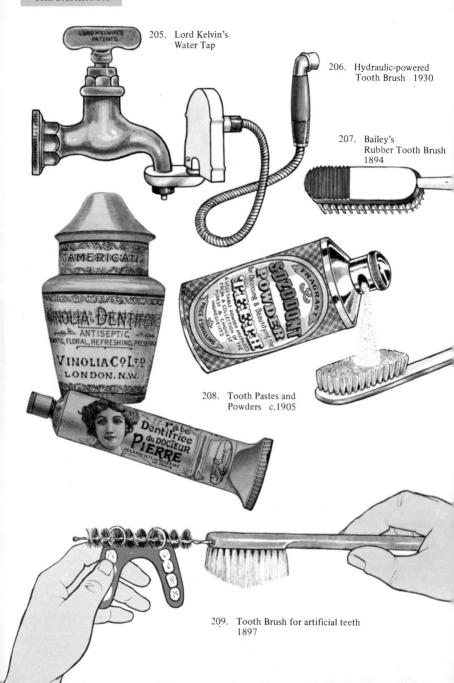

205. Lord Kelvin's Water Tap

206. Hydraulic-powered Tooth Brush 1930

207. Bailey's Rubber Tooth Brush 1894

208. Tooth Pastes and Powders c.1905

209. Tooth Brush for artificial teeth 1897

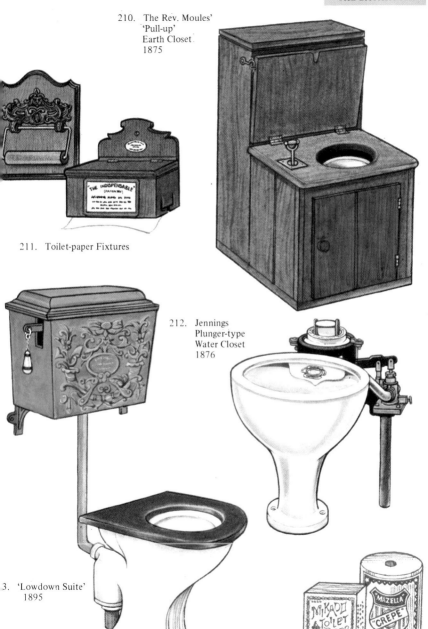

210. The Rev. Moules'
'Pull-up'
Earth Closet
1875

211. Toilet-paper Fixtures

212. Jennings
Plunger-type
Water Closet
1876

3. 'Lowdown Suite'
1895

214. 'The New Humber'
1890

215. 'Deluge' Pedestal
c.1890

216. Brass Bedstead with
     Wire wove mattress
     1883

217. 'Servant's
     Press Bedstead'
     1896

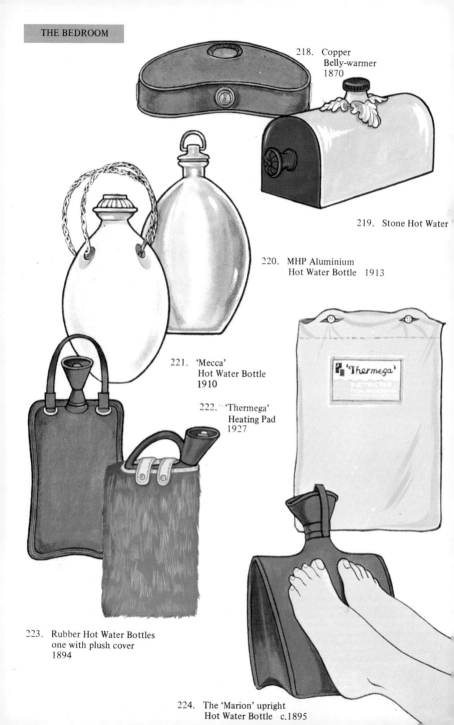

218. Copper Belly-warmer 1870

219. Stone Hot Water

220. MHP Aluminium Hot Water Bottle 1913

221. 'Mecca' Hot Water Bottle 1910

222. 'Thermega' Heating Pad 1927

223. Rubber Hot Water Bottles one with plush cover 1894

224. The 'Marion' upright Hot Water Bottle c.1895

225. Clarke's 'Pyramid' Food Warmer
with Bed-tray

226. Clarke's 'Pyramid'
Night-light Watch-holder
c.1890

227. Clarke's 'Pyramid'
Nursery Lamp Food Warmer

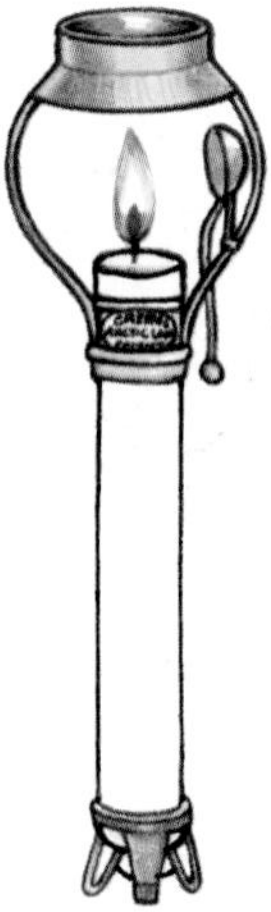

228. 'Arctic' Candle Lamp
1895

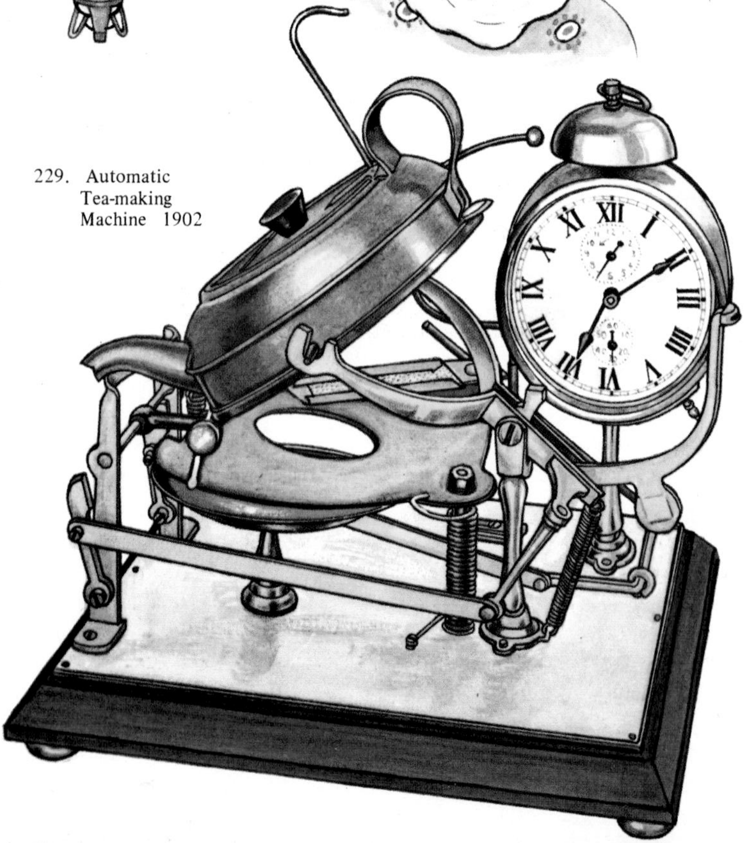

229. Automatic
Tea-making
Machine 1902

230. Swiss 8-day
Electric Clock
c.1913

231. Electric
Ceiling Clock
c.1913

232. 'Time-o'-Night' Watch Illuminator
c.1913

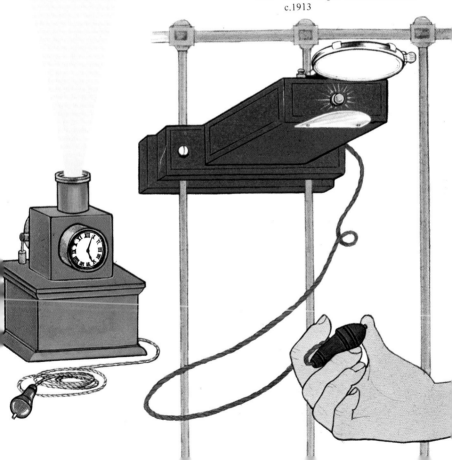

233. Scent Sprays 1907

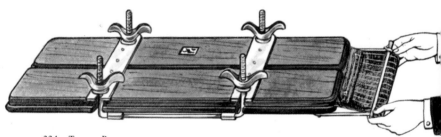

234. Trouser Press

235. Shoe Tree

236. 'Queen Mab' Perfume
   Vaporizing Lamp
   1885

237. Electric Hair Dryer
c.1925

CURL YOUR HAIR!

238. Electro-magnetic
Curling Comb c.1870

239. 'The Princess' Hair Dryer
and Burnisher 1895

240. Automatic Hair Waver
and Curler 1892

241. Hinde's
Hair Curler

HINDE'S PATENT
HAIR CURLERS
OF THE BOX OF FOUR

HINDES CURLERS

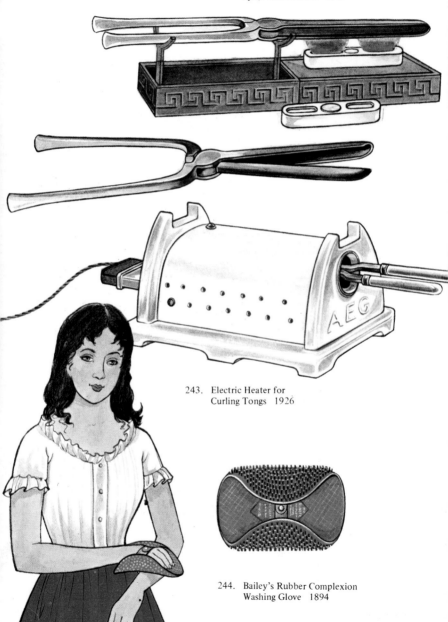

242. Curling Tongs and
Spirit Stove Heater 1907

243. Electric Heater for
Curling Tongs 1926

244. Bailey's Rubber Complexion
Washing Glove 1894

245. Budding's Lawn Mower 1830

6. 'New Easy' Lawn Mower 1890

247. 'New Excelsior' Lawn Mower 1874

248. Ransome's 'New Automaton' Lawn Mower c.1890

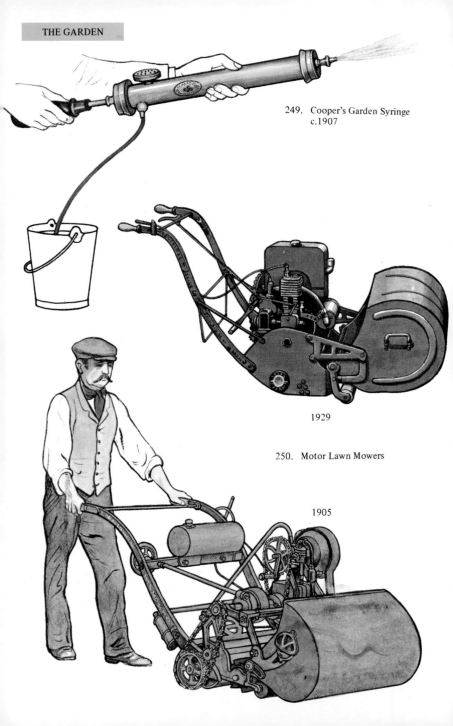

249. Cooper's Garden Syringe
c.1907

1929

250. Motor Lawn Mowers

1905

251. Merryweather Watering Hose
     1900

MERRYWEATHER AND SONS

252. 'Twin Comet'
     Lawn Sprinkler 1887

253. Ridgeway's
     Hedge Cutter
     1885

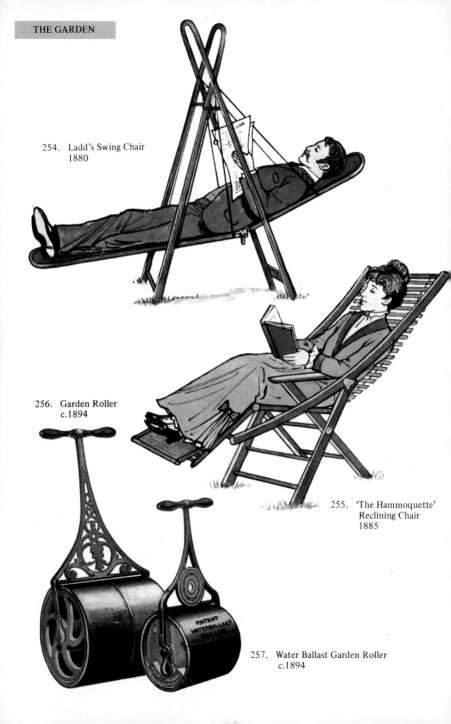

254. Ladd's Swing Chair
1880

256. Garden Roller
c.1894

255. 'The Hammoquette'
Reclining Chair
1885

257. Water Ballast Garden Roller
c.1894

258. Bell's Combined
     Transmitter and Receiver
     1877

TELEPHONES

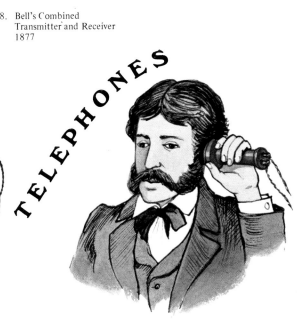

260. Gower-Bell Telephone
     1880

Crossley Carbon Pencil Telephone   1880

261. Ericsson Table Telephone
1895

262. Wall Telephone
c.1900

263. 'Candlestick'
Telephone 1924

264. Plastic Handset
Telephone 1929

265. Bell Indicator c.1900

266. Clarke's 'Pyramid' Night Light Lamp with Bracket 1894

267. 'Norton' Door Check

268. Portiere, shown without Curtain

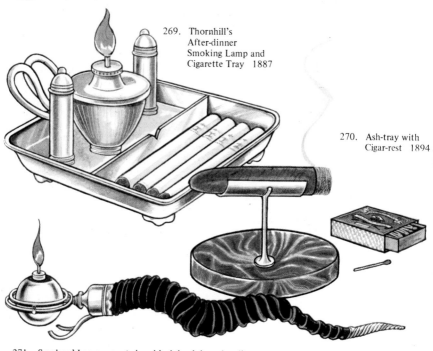

269. Thornhill's
After-dinner
Smoking Lamp and
Cigarette Tray   1887

270.   Ash-tray with
Cigar-rest   1894

271.   Smokers' Lamp mounted on black buck-horn handle.
c.1907

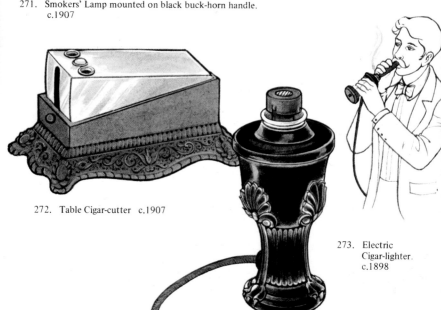

272.   Table Cigar-cutter   c.1907

273.   Electric
Cigar-lighter.
c.1898

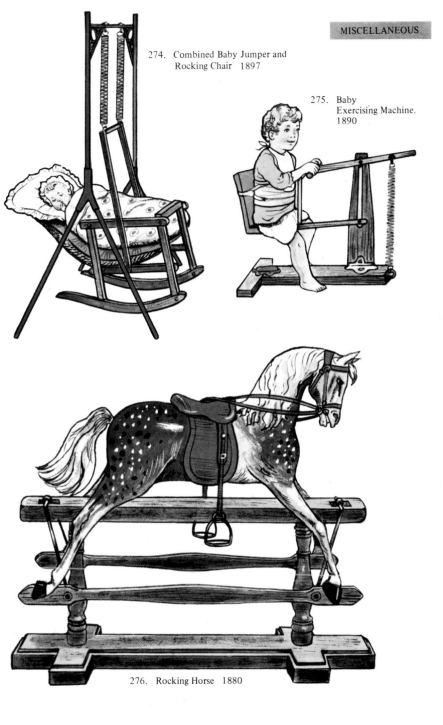

274. Combined Baby Jumper and Rocking Chair 1897

275. Baby Exercising Machine. 1890

276. Rocking Horse 1880

277. Dr. Scott's Electric Flesh Brush

278. 'Horse Exercise at Home' c.1896

COPPER

FELT

ZINC

279. Electro-magnetic Hair Brush

The clothes tub above was pivoted on a horizontal axis and was rotated by hand. The 'steam' mentioned in the name only referred to the kind which might rise off the hot water, and not to any steam-driven tumbler. Another exception was the machine produced in Germany by the firm of Krauss (59). Their 1923 model had a coal fire fitted under the galvanised boiler with its own flue to carry away the smoke. The tumbling motion was achieved either with the removable crank handle provided, or with a neat factory modification using one of Krauss' own electric motors with an automatic reversing mechanism. The action of this gear seems particularly violent and broadly resembles throwing a car from top into reverse at regular intervals. Within a couple of years of its appearance, an electric water heater would have been available, but 1923 was too early for powerful units to be considered an economic solution for domestic machines. In the meantime the owner of a Krauss machine had to put up with the coal, soot, smuts and ashes in the same room as the washing.

An interesting washer/spin-drier was made c. 1924 by the Savage Arms Corporation of Utica, N.Y. It had a $\frac{1}{4}$ horsepower built-in motor which drove the tub through gears at a slow speed for washing and at a higher speed for spin-drying. In its washing position the tub was inclined at an angle which let it dip in the water, then at the end of the desired washing time, the water was let out through a drain plug at the bottom and the tub manually lifted (full of wet clothes) off its driving spindle and repositioned on a vertical one. This then drove the tub in the upright mode at a much faster speed, expelling the water by centrifugal force.

In a large household the weekly wash was a full-time occupation and was the responsibility of the laundry maid. She had to sort the dirty clothes on a Saturday, separating them into sheets and linen in one heap, muslins and fine things in another, and cotton and woollen clothes in a third. Heavily soiled clothes were soaked all day Sunday, lighter ones just overnight, until the wash began around five o'clock on Monday morning. With cook spending all her time getting hot water, there was usually a cold lunch that day. Clothes were hung out to dry on Monday and Tuesday or draped over a wooden clothes-horse that was hauled up to the ceiling to benefit from the hot air rising, and also to get it out of the way. On Wednesday the wash was folded ready for mangling and ironing on Thursday and Friday. And on Saturday it all began again!

Mangling dates back to around the beginning of the eighteenth century and we can see that as it followed the drying period it was not used to force out water but to iron linen smooth. Early mangles made use of considerable pressure and often included a built-in linen press, an upper board being wound down towards a lower one with a large wooden screw. Tindall's Scotch Mangle of 1850 had three rollers on top of each other, and the sheets were fed in succession through both gaps getting a double nip for every rotation of the roller. Then they got a final pressing in the linen press at the bottom.

An alternative was the box mangle and one could be found in many large households of the mid-nineteenth century. It had a big wooden box about 6 feet long which was filled with stones to weigh it down. Clothes were folded and wound round thick wooden rollers which were then inserted below the box. The crank handle was turned and the box would slowly trundle backwards and forwards over the clothes. Getting the big box moving was the hard part because of its enormous weight, but a large fly-wheel on the back helped sustain the motion. It had a built-in lifting device so the rollers could be easily removed. Bradford's box mangles cost £12 in 1864.

Though the various mangles were basically for smoothing and pressing, there were smaller models known as wringers used for expelling water as soon as the clothes were lifted out of the tub. By the use of a screw and spring device on many models, it was possible to alter the pressure of the rollers, and therefore use the machine for either wringing or mangling. Some were made to bolt on to the washing machine or the edge of a table, while others came with their own cast iron stands. This market was well supplied with manufacturers such as Ewbank and Bradford (56,57), whose machines sold for around £2 in the first decade of the twentieth century.

Articles of linen could conveniently be mangled but more complex shapes such as clothing were pressed with heated irons. By 1851 the laundry maid had three types of iron available. The first one was the hollow metal box iron (62) with a lift-up door on the back. A slug of cast iron a little smaller but approximately the same shape as the box was put in the fire grate until it glowed red hot, and then taken out with tongs and slipped into the iron. They were in use throughout the nineteenth century.

The second type was also a hollow metal box, but this time filled with glowing coals from the fire (65). To raise the temperature the maid had to insert a pair of bellows into a hole in the back of the iron and pump madly. However, it had the disarming knack of sending a shower of soot and ashes out of the chimney at the front all over the freshly washed clothes.

The third type was the simple flat iron (63) or sad-iron made of solid cast iron ('sad' means heavy) which was heated either on the kitchen stove or else on a special laundry stove. The iron from the kitchen stove would be dirty and so required cleaning on paper before using, whereas the irons from the laundry stove never came into direct contact with ashes or flames and so remained clean. Never satisfied, there were also sad-irons with built-in spirit stoves (70) using the same system as a decorator's paint-stripping blow-lamp. An alternative method of heating was by installing a gas burner inside the iron (71) on the end of a flexible pipe, as in the Bolgiano Manufacturing Company's model of 1894 which they claimed 'gets hot in 5 minutes'.

Sad-irons came in many different sizes, were usually heavy to lift and too hot to hold comfortably. Like washing dishes, ironing has a special place in many housewives' black books so you will not be surprised to discover one of the first major improvements was made by a woman. Mrs Potts patented her iron in 1871 and although they were still heavy they had a clip-on walnut handle which didn't get hot (64). It could be transferred from iron to iron, one of which would be in use while a couple of others were heating up on the fire. They were sold by the Enterprise Manufacturing Company in sets of three with one handle, a trivet to stand the hot iron on, plus a 'little girl's iron and its own handle', at $4.50 the set in 1890. A little detail like the iron for a child can only have been suggested by a woman who knew the problem of keeping children occupied while work had to be done.

Anything that could ease the drudgery of heating numerous flat irons, avoid using different weights and finishes for different stages of the job, and lessen the discomfort and heat, could not help but be a success. And so it was. Electric irons (*67,68*) came on the market in 1890 at about the same time as the folding ironing-board. One early French model (*66*) was heated by an electric arc between two half-inch diameter carbon rods of the type used in arc-lamps in the 1860s. But the rods were continuously burnt away and so needed forever adjusting to keep the correct gap. At the same time it shed white-hot pieces of carbon into the body of the iron. All in all the iron was lethal and gave way to a sounder model using a heated sole-plate on the same lines as the electric cooker's boiling ring. These were made in England as early as 1891 by Crompton's and were popular with households who had installed electric lighting. This was because they could be plugged into a light socket and so be used for next to nothing in the same way as early electric kettles.

Within the next twenty years more and more companies manufactured electric irons as they were such good sellers. In 1909 an advertisement for Westinghouse Inc. showed a picture of a man sweating uncomfortably in his office. To emphasise the point the room was being heated by a large cast-iron stove. The copy line ran: 'Put a stove in your office and build a good rousing fire in it. It will give you some idea of the heat your wife has to endure every time she irons. You think it's hot do you? Then what does your wife think while ironing to the accompaniment of a hot stove. Why not kick out that stove and get her a Westinghouse Electric Iron?' They did not want to minimise the effect of making the American male feel really guilty by describing any technical details, and anyway that might frighten off the American female. But if the same advertisement had appeared in Britain in 1909, then doubtless for 'your wife' it would have read 'your maid'.

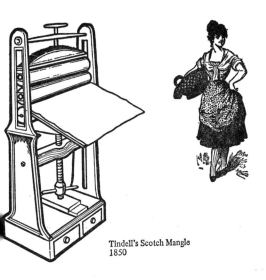

Tindell's Scotch Mangle
1850

'Red Star'
Hand-operated
Washing Machine
c.1914

Washer and
Spin drier
1924

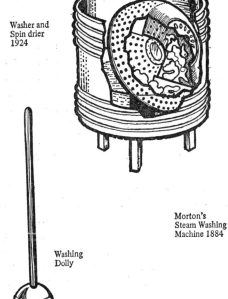

Morton's
Steam Washing
Machine 1884

Washing
Dolly

2

Living Rooms

The term 'living rooms' is here used to describe the public rooms of a house. The lounge, sitting room or parlour all describe the same room for relaxing in. We shall also cover in this chapter the study and the dining room.

Carpet sweepers and vacuum cleaners

In order that cleanliness should remain next to godliness, the Victorians had a wonderful solution, the housemaid! Among her many duties, she had to keep the place clean. This required daily sweeping and dusting, but try as she might, the job was never really finished. Much of the dust was only raised and of course it gradually resettled somewhere else. The same problem had been affecting Mr Bissell, a china shop owner of Grand Rapids, Michigan, who found he was allergic to dust which came from the straw used for packing the china. So in 1876 he built a carpet sweeper which he called the 'Grand Rapids' (75). This hand-operated machine was excellent and became widely known all over the Western world, and for the next twenty-five years no alternative method of cleaning was invented. The original design was well thought out and has remained in production virtually unchanged for the last hundred years.

In 1901 a compressed air device was demonstrated at St Pancras Station, London, for cleaning a carriage belonging to the Midland Railway, but because it worked by blowing, it only succeeded in repeating the housemaid's problem of raising the dust without getting rid of it. Fortunately for all future generations of housemaids, there was a Mr Hubert Cecil Booth in the audience who recognised this basic error. Discussing the subject afterwards, Booth suggested that sucking rather than blowing was the answer, and proceeded to demonstrate his theory by placing his handkerchief on the arm of his chair and sucking through it. On lifting it up he revealed a patch of dust on the underside of the cloth, and having convinced himself that this simple but effective system worked, he went away to make a mechanical version. It contained a pump and filter to replace his breath and handkerchief, and following a trial in his office, he patented his new invention on 30 August 1901. This, the vacuum cleaner, was the first real alternative to Bissell's carpet sweeper.

Booth then set up the British Vacuum Cleaner Company, not for selling machines, but for going round to customers and doing their cleaning for them. His uniformed employees would arrive at a house with a horse-drawn van containing a petrol-driven vacuum pump and several hundred feet of flexible hose (73). This was so they could reach all parts of the house, even if the hoses had to be passed through a first-floor window, as sometimes happened where the ground floor was occupied by a shop. These activities caused quite a stir in fashionable London society, so much so that it was considered a very clever thing when a tea party was thrown to entertain the guests by having Booth's men in to clean the room in which they were sitting. With the notable exception of Buckingham Palace and Windsor Castle (who they could hardly refuse), the BVC provided their cleaning service without selling a single vacuum cleaner until 1906.

In the meantime various rivals were trying to cash in on this very lucrative market by selling household vacuum cleaners which did not require a large engine to run them and so avoided the horse-and-cart end of the machine. In answer to this threat, Booth produced the Trolley Vac in 1906 (74), a heavy box on wheels containing a sophisticated electric motor and pump which could be run off a light socket. To prove to the sceptical owner that it was doing its job, the hose included a short length of glass tube so the dust could be seen as it was sucked up. Selling at 35 guineas, the Trolley Vac came complete with half a dozen different attachments, and its own booklet with a dramatic 'before and after' illustration of a brightly coloured carpet being magically revealed where the nozzle had just cleaned. An early advertising poster by the artist John Hassall, R.A., confused the buyers with its slogan 'Help'. Was this an offer of help, or a strangled cry from a frightened servant who was being attacked by the machine? Three years later in 1909, Hassall repaired the damage by drawing a similar poster with the message 'Friends'.

The disadvantage of the Trolley Vac was that it weighed nearly a hundredweight so it was hardly suited to being hauled up and down stairs by a chambermaid. And those rival machines were no better. Avoiding the expensive electric motor, they all required one person to operate a set of bellows and a second person to go around with the hose doing the cleaning. Fortunately a little problem like that didn't worry the English because domestic labour was cheap. Strange models appeared such as the 'Griffith' foot-operated vacuum cleaner of 1905 (*76*), which had a pair of coupled bellows pumped by walking up and down on them. It also had one of those sections of glass in the hose. Sir Hiram Maxim designed another variation (*78*) which was worked by rocking a handle backwards and forwards, the dust being removed through a filter of sawdust. It sold at 5 guineas in 1909. The 'Baby Daisy' (*80*) was a similar rival, worked by a broom handle fixed to a pair of bellows which cost £4 in 1904 and rapidly became one of the most popular models. Not to be outdone, Booth stepped into the field with his own two-operative machine which he called the 'Hand Excelsior'. Selling at 7 guineas in 1911, its pair of bellows were worked by turning a crank handle. The 'Wizard' (*77*) by Maguire and Catchell of Dublin followed in 1912 on very similar lines. There was even the American model which attempted to take the drudgery out of pumping the handle to and fro, by building the bellows into a rocking-chair! While grandfather swayed contentedly backwards and forwards, the diligent housewife glided round the carpet with the nozzle sucking up the dust.

It was clear the vacuum cleaner was a little labour-intensive at this stage, and the time for the one-operative machine had come. The first hand-powered models resembled overgrown bicycle pumps, either with the pump part inside, or, as with the 'Star' (*79*), the longer circular bellows outside. They were difficult to use because you had to keep the nozzle on the floor while pumping madly with the other hand. Nevertheless, the shortage of domestics in America meant this type of machine had a receptive market. It also followed that if a large market could be assured, then a one-man machine could be mass-produced that would have the edge on all its predecessors. With this in mind a Mr Spangler of Ohio set to work. His machine would be light and manageable and, like Booth's original Trolley Vac, have an electric motor. It was in 1907 when he made his first prototype out of a tin can, a broomstick, an old flour sack, and an electric motor to drive his pump. That sack was used as an external dust bag, a feature we have come to recognise in modern vacuum cleaners. The machine was excellent and the name Spangler seemed destined for fame and fortune. Well, he sold the rights to a leather manufacturer, who produced the first commercial model in 1908 (*82*). Even at the high price of $75 (about £25) it achieved a remarkable success, so much so that the leather business was dropped in favour of all-out production on the vacuum cleaner. By 1912 they were even exporting to Europe, and by the mid-1920s 'Spanglering' had become big business, except that nobody called it that. They called it after the leather manufacturer, whose name was W. Hoover. A pity. Spanglering sounds so much more glamorous than hoovering.

Hoover's prices dropped as their sales went up, but in such a lucrative business it wasn't long before the competition started. In London there was the 'Magic' (*84*) selling at £7/10/- in 1915. Then there was the 'Air Way' (*81*) in America, which not only vacuum cleaned via the floor nozzle, but if desired could suck through the handle grip and clean down the sides of armchairs. Its air flow could also be reversed to work a hair-dryer! In much the same way firms like Electrolux, who introduced the horizontal canister-type of machine in the 1920s, were later to offer a paint spray gun as a free gift. The canister contained the dust bag and motor, and unlike the type that lay on the floor, the early models were built as one solid unit, though there was a sling provided to take the weight over your shoulder. The Model 10 with the pistol grip was on sale in 1927.

Heating

When it came to room heating, coal fires were favourite. After all, since the seventeenth century coal had been the main fuel and as long as it remained cheap and there were plenty of servants to carry the coal scuttles, it was of little consequence that the fireplaces were inefficient or unnecessarily large. There had been improvements made by the American-born Count Rumford, who in 1796 designed a modification which could be built into an existing fireplace. He bricked up most of the opening and sloped the upper part of the fire-back which threw the heat out into the room. He also cut down the chimney throat to a slit about 4 inches deep which improved the air flow and stopped smoke being blown down the flue.

In Germany and Russia it was more common to have a free-standing stove in the corner of a room with a flue feeding the smoke through the wall into a chimney. They did not agree with the English preoccupation for visible flames, and fires in these cases were more a source of heat than a focus of attention. Each room had its own stove, often 6 feet high and 2 feet round, and like the kitchen range it usually had a hob to keep a kettle hot. The stove was clad in decorative ceramic tiles or sometimes metal covered in wood painted to look like tiles. Some even had a drawer built into the top above the flue and so formed a simple if small airing cupboard. By 1880 the more ornate stoves were made of cast iron fretwork, the spaces being filled with coloured glass. A German model of this period (86) by Junkers and Ruh of Karlsruhe had doors at two different levels on three of its four sides. There was a small hotplate above the flue outlet on the back, and the top of the stove was crowned with a winged cherub which could be slid aside to reveal another hotplate.

Around the turn of the century simpler smaller stoves became fashionable such as the 'Egg' (88) by Humber Stove Works, and the 'Sigma' (89) by the Carron Iron Foundry in Scotland. If you were not a dab hand at fire lighting with those twisted knots of newspaper then the 'Queen' fire-lighting fan (85) of 1898 was clearly for you. It had a clockwork-driven fan which you wound up with a bent metal key. A burning rag soaked in lamp oil was inserted in the hole at the end of a pipe and its flames would be blown into the fire to get it going. Once consumed the rag burnt out, but the draught continued fanning the flames until the motor ran down. You could even hook the fan on to the firebars using the same piece of bent metal that served as a key.

With the discovery of oil in Pennsylvania in 1859, a cheap source of kerosine or paraffin was assured, and the sale of lamps and heaters dramatically increased. Before that, animal and vegetable oils had been widely used but were inferior to the new fuel. Nowadays we think of engines as the prime consumers of oil, but in 1860 it was lighting, and the American product was exported all over Europe in tins packed in wooden boxes. Towards the end of the century, ornate cast iron tracery surrounds were very popular for fires, a style that was copied by both solid fuel and gas fire manufacturers. The stove had a larger metal chimney built round the tall glass cylinder which provided it with a column of air to heat. It was soon realised that tinted glass inserts looked very attractive (and as we have noted were later adopted for solid fuel stoves as well). The 'Lily' (*93*) by Harpers of Willenhall was an impressive architectural design with elongated gothic windows on the sides filled with ruby glass. It was a stove-enamelled cast iron fire with two flat wicks and a removable top so it could be used to cook on. Ruby glass was also used in the Albion heater (*94*), which though smooth on the outside was dimpled on the inside, a detail which was only obvious when the fire was burning. An alternative design to the enclosed column oil stove, was an open-fronted fire with a beaten reflector, usually of copper; the 'Ardent' (*91*) was a variation that was completely open but had a table fitted above it, and even a towel rail around the edges. It boasted 120 candle power and cost 2 guineas in 1907. Other ornate designs of the 1890s came from firms such as Veritas and Rippingille (*95*). Clark's Hygienic Syphon Stove (*102*), patented in 1881, was designed to be run on either oil or gas. It consumed 2 pints of paraffin in eight hours.

Gas fires did not become a reality until about 1880, long after the first effective gas cookers and geysers, and made little headway against the open coal fire until the end of the century, yet they had been suggested by John Maiben as early as 1813. The gas flame by itself did not offer a great deal of warmth or comfort, but when it was played on a surface that would glow white hot, the effect was much better. The first radiants were made in 1882 of tufted asbestos (*97*), protruding about the depth of a toothbrush bristle and trapped between fireclay bricks, as can be seen in the Fletcher Warrington fire with its conical chimney. A better material was fireclay, which although fragile was easy to replace. It was made in a variety of shapes from 1905, some like small stones known as patent ball fuel (*96*), some in short stubby columns as in the Carron gas fire of 1910 (*99*), others with the more familiar type of fretwork column, and the latest, a more geometric grid form introduced in 1925.

Ornate cast iron was the most common material for the fire surround as in the 'Omega' (*103*) of 1900, though there were even models where the burner was placed inside a glazed earthenware pot. These had fireclay radiants fixed to the underside of the lid and acted as a convector heater. The connection to the gas tap was usually flexible and when long enough could be fitted to a special adaptor to the gas light (*98*). After all, in 1880 almost every town house had gas lighting, but not necessarily gas taps at fire level.

For the 'real fire' fanatics, the very latest thing was the 'log fire' with a built-in flicker. We usually associate this with electric fires (*111*), for which the 'Magicoal' effect was patented as early as 1915, but there was also a gas version available in the 1920s. It had two sets of burners; the first played on a group of fireclay logs raising them to incandescence, while the other set fed a series of small non-aerated burners which flickered as they sucked in air. One model, the 'Metro', came complete with fake Tudor fire-dogs on either side of the basket of logs.

The best way to encourage the use of electricity, was to develop gadgets and appliances that ran on electricity. This in turn required laying wiring in houses, a job that gave lots of work to carpenters because they would cover it all in wooden trunking. With the housing boom that followed the First World War the practice began of building in power supplies as well as lighting. Fires were widely available by this time and it was argued that if power points were built in there would be no need for fireplaces and chimneys. They only took up valuable space, increased building costs, and were the cause of most of the dust that the housemaid worked hard to get rid of. It was even suggested that cheap electricity would permit a return to the pre-Victorian golden age of the thriving cottage industries which had disappeared with the introduction of the steam engine! But people were not so keen to give up their open fires as the electricity companies had hoped, maybe because the elements on early electric fires did not glow. In the late 1890s electric fires worked the same way as those early cooker hobs. They were the same cast-iron plates fixed in an upright frame. A 12-inch square model (*105*) in 1897 by Crompton Ltd costing £3/10/- was fitted with a regulating switch 'by means of which the heat can be controlled to a nicety', so the catalogue said. The wires were embedded in enamel and bonded to the back of the plate, and the whole thing was mounted on an ornate metal screen to put in front of the coal fire. Other models used elongated light bulbs, about 2 inches round and 8 inches long fitted in a row in front of a polished reflector. These were the invention of Mr H. J. Dowsing in 1896 and gave out both heat and light. It wasn't quite the rival for the open fire but at least it was visible heat. To get some idea of how hot they were, each bulb produced about two and a half times what a normal 100-watt light bulb gives out now. (It is not such a bad idea because the tungsten light bulb, which dates from 1911, is really a very efficient heat source.) The Carron bulb fire (*104*) uses four Dowsing lamps and dates from about 1904. Dowsing Bulbs were frosted on the outside to cut down the amount of light, but the reflector behind them had to be redesigned because it had the annoying habit of focusing the heat rays back on the bulb which caused the filament to sag and disintegrate and in extreme cases even melt the glass. But that was put right in 1917 with a new shaped reflector. Perhaps the nicest model using a Dowsing Bulb was the Tricity Sun Ray Lamp of 1927 (*124*) which was shaped like a standard lamp with the shade made from copper reflectors. Using a clear bulb it doubled as a light and a fire!

The year 1906 was the breakthrough date for electric fires though, because in January of that year Mr L. Marsh of Illinois solved the problem of that iron resistance wire which was normally used. Firstly it rusted on contact with the atmosphere, and secondly it didn't like being heated up and cooled down too often, which was a bit of a nuisance considering that the whole point of the electric fire was that it could be switched on or off at will, unlike the coal fire. Mr Marsh used a new metal made of nickel and chrome which was unaffected by the atmosphere and far outlasted all the earlier alternatives. It meant a fire could now have a wire element which did not need protecting and so could be seen glowing.

In September of 1908 Mr C. O. Bastian patented an invention which was designed to circumvent the payment of royalties to Mr Marsh and his nichrome wire. By encasing a wire element in a quartz tube of some ⅜ inch diameter, Bastian tubes were protected from the atmosphere and so could be made of iron, or nickel or silver. The Quartzalite fire (106) of 1909 is a model using these elements, though they were fragile and marked easily, hence its protective cage.

In 1912 Mr C. R. Belling invented a fireclay former which would take a nichrome (as the nickle-chrome alloy was called) wire wound backwards and forwards over it, and the whole thing could be raised almost to incandescence like the gas radiants. He designed an electric fire that same year and started production in his garden shed in London. Belling's 'Standard' fire (108) sold so well he dropped both an electric kettle and immersion heater from his catalogue the following year to concentrate solely on his money-spinner. One of the extras was a peg at the top of the fire to hang a kettle from, and an attachment that could hold bread for toasting. Electric fires could now offer several distinct advantages—they were pollution free, their heat was available within seconds of switching them on, the heat was not wasted up the chimney, and they were labour saving. It is not so surprising that domestic servants were easier to convince than their employers of the merits of the electric fire because it saved them doing all that blackleading, sifting ashes and carrying coal! Yet oddly enough as late as 1926 a team of Scottish experts, all of them electrical engineers, still doubted the value of an all-electric house because of (1) the high running costs, (2) the 'real fire' obsession and (3) the problem of disposing of refuse, mainly garbage, which would otherwise have been thrown on the fire. It leads one to consider if the electric fire in the living room and the electric cooker in the kitchen were responsible for the introduction of the waste-paper basket and the pedal-bin.

Lighting

Although by 1900 there were several different methods of lighting available, it should not be forgotten that many houses still used a large quantity of candles, and all the trappings like candle-holders and snuffers were still common gadgets.

To get a better reading light, for instance, there were hoods made to fit round candlesticks which reflected the light in one direction only. They had nickel-plated surfaces and could be slid up and down to keep the flame at the focus of the reflector. There was a way to get over the problem of different diameter holes in the top of candle-holders too. All you needed was a 'Pola lite' Candle Tube. This held a spring-mounted candle which kept the flame at the same height even though the length of wax changed as it melted away. It had a brass tube with an adjustable foot. This was a rubber bush which would expand or contract when twisted, in the same way as some thermos flask stoppers fit nowadays. There was even a metal support on top which took any number of different shades according to your taste.

Oil lamps had been in use for at least 4,000 years in some form or another, the kind we recognise today with the tall glass chimney being a development of the Swiss-born Ami Argand in 1784. Until petroleum (the source of paraffin) was discovered in Pennsylvania in 1859, they burnt vegetable oils such as olive and rape-seed oil, or imported mineral oil from Burma. Their advantage over the candle was the steadier flame and greater light, but they also gave out a certain amount of heat which drew up dust and darkened the ceilings. Compared with simple oil lamps which had a small rope-like wick, the Argand type had an open circular wick that allowed air to rise through the centre and improve the combustion. This in turn gave a better light, and produced less smoke, but it also used more oil and so caused the lamps to be limited to wealthier families. However, in the 1860s cheap paraffin replaced the more expensive oils and this restriction was eased.

There were table models (*114,115*), wall bracket models (*116*), hanging models and others built into furniture, but all of them required frequent cleaning if they were to give off a smokeless light. One long lasting design was the student or reading lamp (*117*), which first appeared in the early nineteenth century for burning rape-seed (colza) oil. With minor modifications for burning paraffin, the lamp was still a popular model eighty years later. It was sold by the Army and Navy stores for 12/8d. in 1907. Another gas lamp, the Albo Carbon lamp of 1885 (119), actually gave much of its illumination due to impurities in the gas. It had camphor balls in the lower reservoir which gradually volatised with the heat from the burners and gave the right type of impurity to increase the light level, compared with lamps burning pure town gas.

The Veritas Lamp Works of London produced a ceiling-mounted oil lamp with a sliding suspension (113) which allowed you to pull it down closer to the table for reading or to leave it up at the ceiling for a general level of illumination. This model cost £2/8/– in 1893. The sliding suspension had been used earlier on gas lamps (121) though these had the extra problem of the possible leakage of gas, which was usually prevented by using a water seal.

Gas lighting had been used in England since the beginning of the nineteenth century to illuminate streets after dark, starting in London in 1807 and supplying fifty-one towns by 1823. Abroad it reached Baltimore in 1816, Paris in 1819, Berlin in 1826, New York in 1837 and Moscow in 1866. By 1840 gas moved indoors. It was used in well-off households to light hallways and the living rooms but with improvements in cost and efficiency became a common illuminant in most houses by 1870. To rival the candle-burning chandeliers, there were many-flame fittings known as gasoliers (and following the same trend later, even electroliers!), but the heat given off could be stifling; incidentally in poorer houses in the early twentieth century gas lighting was preferred to electricity because of the extra heat which cost nothing. But gas lights weren't very reliable and often only gave a moderate amount of illumination. The solution rested with the use of a material which could be heated to incandescence, and was provided in 1887 by the Austrian Carl von Welsbach. He invented the gas mantle (118) which when fixed over a gas jet improved the light output at least three times. He had spent several years investigating incandescence and by February 1887 was confident enough to exhibit his mantle at an exhibition in London. Both *The*

Times and the *Financial Times* reported on his lamp and in the same year he set up a factory in Westminster which made both burners and mantles, a guinea for the former and the incredibly high price of 5/– for the latter. However, by the early 1890s the mantles were selling well and apart from their initially high cost were proving to be a great success. Besides, in 1889, the 'Penny-in-the-slot' meter had been invented which meant gas could be paid for according to one's pocket—which was a Victorian way of letting the working class have gas in their homes without the distasteful problem of running up enormous unpayable bills. And what a boon to the landlord of the rooming house.

There was a basic fault with the gas mantle that took some years to solve, and when that finally did happen it was really too late. The mantle sat *above* the flame. Now that meant that the gas pipe and cock was below it and obscured quite a lot of the light from where it was wanted most, i.e. below. It took von Welsbach until 1905 to perfect the inverted mantle, which was twice as bright as its predecessor and twenty times better than a candle, but there was now another alternative method of lighting available and it caused the death of the gas lighting industry.

In 1878 the American Mr Thomas Edison and the English Mr Swan both independently produced a successful electric incandescent filament lamp. Their aim had been to provide a much more manageable amount of light than the brilliant carbon arc lamps of the 1860s, which anyway were unsuitable for domestic use because of their tendency to shed pieces of white-hot carbon. The topic had been looked at for some time, and a committee of prominent scientists finally announced their verdict to the British Parliament in 1878 stating: 'The sub-division of the electric light is a problem that cannot be solved by the human brain'. And to be proved wrong, twice within the same year, how degrading! After some confusion between Edison and Swan as to who was the first inventor, they agreed to forget their differences and in the interests of science (and profit) joined forces in 1881 to become the Edison and Swan United Electric Light Company. They manufactured a new light source for the home that was silent, clean, constant and efficient, compared with the gas

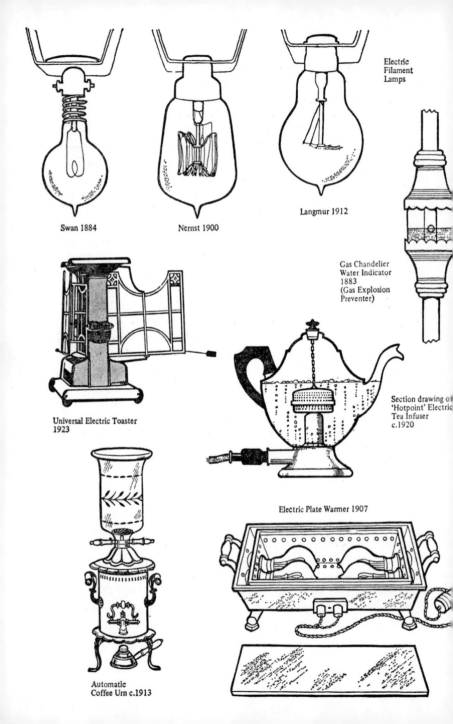

Electric Filament Lamps

Swan 1884

Nernst 1900

Langmur 1912

Gas Chandelier Water Indicator 1883 (Gas Explosion Preventer)

Universal Electric Toaster 1923

Section drawing of 'Hotpoint' Electric Tea Infuser c.1920

Electric Plate Warmer 1907

Automatic Coffee Urn c.1913

light which was noisy and oil-lamps which were sooty and if not frequently cleaned, smelly. The filament lamp was none of these; not only was it much brighter, but it was also safer than the naked flame. In the early days very few people had electricity, but the light bulb was an instant success and soon changed the picture. By the time the inverted mantle was on sale, electric lighting had been available for over a quarter of a century and gas lighting never again topped the market. The electric lamp took all the forms known earlier in gas lamps (*122–125*), from the ceiling rose to wall bracket and on to portable battery-run lamps like the 14/6d. hand-held battery lamp by Ever Ready (*126*).

The vacuum in the early bulbs was not particularly good so the filament actually burnt, and gradually got thinner as it vaporised. At the same time this blackened the inside of the glass and reduced its efficiency as a light. Later pumps produced a more complete vacuum and so this problem was solved. It took until 1911 to perfect the tungsten filament used today, all manner of alternatives having been used before then, including cardboard and artificial silk. To get some idea of the public's acceptance of the electric light, there was an Automatic Bulb Machine made in 1917 which produced 2,500 units an hour. Ten years later it was necessary to develop a new machine which produced 60,000 bulbs an hour in order to satisfy the demand. Gas lighting faded away into the background in the face of this sort of opposition, but there was one small consolation. They realised that it was the *heat* which raised the gas mantle to incandescence, and as a light source it was not so great, so from the 1920s onwards the gas companies concentrated on fires and cookers and succeeded in cornering about 70 per cent of the cooker market by 1935.

Entertainment and relaxation

Gas lighting and later electric lighting did more to improve the habit of reading books than anything before it.

In the late 1880s and 1890s a host of literary aids were available. One of the more ornate versions was the Ohio-made 'Holloway Book-rest and Dictionary Holder' (*128*). Mounted on wheels, it could be positioned next to the seated reader from where he had everything within arm's reach. It had its own table for the reading lamp; a large book rest to take the dictionary or major reference work; a smaller book rest with clips at the bottom to keep your page; and round the stem of the stand were brackets to hold four or five other books. The advertisement had this to say: 'Saves children from the ungraceful and unhealthful habit of bending forward when reading or studying', but it is doubtful whether Father would ever let the Children get near it! A London magazine offered a similar if less ornate model in 1910 called the 'Literary Machine', which only boasted the table and book rest with fitted page clip. Made by Carters of Great Portland Street, it was seen as the companion piece to one of their reclining chairs (*127*), which had a built-in foot-stool and an adjustable back. Their products were intended mainly for invalids, but the sheer luxury can only have encouraged hypochondriacs to stay poorly.

If you were not sitting in a comfortable chair and pretending to be ill, you might play the piano and sing; and there you could use crazy gadgets like automatic music page turners. Each sheet turned by a lever operated by the knee. If you wanted to hear a virtuoso performance on your own piano, then you could feed an automatic piano (*130*) with a roll of paper full of carefully placed perforations. You only had to pedal like mad and pretend to play. A clockwork motor did the rest. Famous composers performed their own works, so you could hear Rhapsody in Blue as Gershwin himself conceived it. Then there were hand organs, miniature versions of the fairground monsters with a motor operating bellows and turning a perforated disc (*133*) or the type that worked like a musical box, hand-cranked as the clockwork motor was not invented until 1895 (*132*). Each disc or cylinder played a different tune, and the machine would be sold for £1 in 1901. The Atlas Organ Company of Camden Town, London, offered easy terms of 4/– monthly, just as they did for their other products. (Their lock-stitch sewing machine, for instance, was 5/– a month or £1/19/–, and guaranteed for four years.) Just three years earlier the first coin-operated phonograph juke-box was on sale, a machine that played back what was on the cylinder whether piano or guitar, rather than just different tunes played on the same organ as in the Nickelodeon.

The phonograph (*135–138*) was another product of the full-time inventor Thomas Alva Edison, who described his work as 'Ninetynine percent perspiration, one percent inspiration'. He invented the principle of the talking machine in 1877 using a hand-turned crank and a tinfoil cylinder, but within a year he had become preoccupied with his work on the electric light bulb, and for some time the phonograph lay gathering dust. Improvements by two others, C. Bell and C. S. Tainter, in the mid-1880s, replaced the tinfoil cylinder with a wax-coated cardboard one, allowing better quality recordings. In the face of their developments Edison rapidly returned to his talking machine and by 1887 his company produced a marketable model. He wrongly believed the demand for such a machine lay in commerce and tried to sell the phonograph as an office dictating machine. Not being able to guarantee what power supply any office might have, Edison covered all possibilities by producing an electric model (battery driven), a water model (driven by a water-powered motor run off the domestic tap) and a treadle model (mounted on a sewing machine base). The reason we do not associate the record player with an office dictating machine today is because it was a commercial failure.

A few of the obsolete machines found their way into people's living rooms and were used for recording and reproducing musical evenings around the parlour piano. Others were bought by travelling exhibitors who showed the machines around the fairs with sometimes as many as seventeen eartubes like stethoscopes in place of the horn. After all you could charge each listener that way, and make others feel they were missing something, which wasn't so easy with a loud-speaker. It took Edison until 1894 to realise there was a future in domestic entertainment and at the same time recognise some of the applications of his machine. Apart from the abortive dictating machine, the phonograph could replay stories, opera, teach languages, record voices of distant relatives, or become the voices of talking dolls and speaking clocks. In the meantime, however, the gramo-phone (*139–142*) had been invented by E. Berliner, a naturalised American of German origin. His disc-playing machine of 1888 opened up the entertainment world, and only played back recordings, it didn't make them. The Gramophone Company hired a talent scout to record top quality artistes at high fees and so brought great music into the homes of many. It was this that made the gramophone acceptable as a musical instrument. Edison finally entered the entertainment arena when he perfected a clockwork motor in 1895 and discontinued all those treadle, water and electric alternatives. His 'Triumph' phonograph sold for $100 (about 20 guineas), but was down to $50 by 1900, five years later. The first HMV gramophone to carry the famous 'dog' trade mark (painted by the artist F. Barraud) was the Gramophone Style No. 5 of 1898 (*141*) and sold for 5 guineas.

If you were to find a recording in French made by the Pathé company between 1906 and 1920, it would be impossible to play except on a Pathé Frères machine. It looks just like an ordinary record, but the sound is backwards. Which is absolutely fine when you realise that their gramophone began playing with the needle in the centre of the disc and worked its way outwards!

Whether disc or cylinder playing, sound quality depended on a good stylus to be changed after each playing, and more important, a large speaker. This meant a bulky cumbersome item requiring a floor support if it was any good, and taking up so much space it was easily knocked over. Naturally it was impossible to keep the dust out of it but the sound quality was hardly Hi-Fi so that was not so disastrous. Machines with built-in horns appeared as early as 1906 when the Victor Company produced its 'Victrola'. Not much had been gained in the way of space because this was a massive piece of furniture. Other models were the Grafonola also of 1906 and the Edison Company's Amberola of 1909. This was their top quality machine, for which they expected the top price of $200.

Phonographs and gramophones had offered a new meaning to the phrase 'home entertainment', and were to be followed by an even more revolutionary invention—the 'wireless'. Guglielmo Marconi had pioneered wireless telegraphy, primarily as a method of communicating with ships at sea, and although both speech and music had been transmitted experimentally as early as 1906, communication was almost exclusively by Morse code until many years later.

The development of the thermionic valve during the First World War made broadcasting possible, though radio communication was a quarter of a century old before regular broadcasting began. Test transmissions which aroused public interest created a market for crystal sets which could receive them. By means of a long outdoor aerial of up to 100 feet (the maximum permitted length) radio signals were picked up from local transmitters built in the centre of big towns, and were listened to through headphones. Crystal sets, like the Gecophone of 1924 (*144*), had no batteries; it was simply the power of the radio waves which moved the diaphragms in the headphones and gave an audible signal. Valve sets needed batteries and gave loudspeaker reproduction, though often only as an extra. The Marconiphone V2 (*143*), for instance, came in the basic form with a set of headphones where a loudspeaker was to be used. A separate amplifier in a similar cabinet was available.

Like gramophones, early radios used a horn-shaped loudspeaker which gave great acoustic advantage and made the maximum use of the feeble power available. The New York-made Thermiodyne (*145*) still used the long outdoor aerial while the contemporary De Forest superhet radio (*147*) had a compact indoor 'frame' aerial which was directional and so could be twisted round to improve reception. It too needed a separate loudspeaker or else a pair of headphones. Apart from the crystal set, all these radios were battery-powered, a perpetual source of trouble and expense, and around 1930 the all-elecric wireless set that plugged into the mains gave a new simplicity to radio listening—as did the single-knob tuning and built-in loudspeaker; the Consolette (*146*) is an example. Throughout this period many people bought kits and built their own sets by following the manufacturer's simple assembly instructions. A real status symbol, mains radios were about ten times as expensive as the earlier crystal sets, retailing at around £17 to £20 in 1932. In Britain the number of yearly licences sold exceeded the five million mark that year. The gramophone could only repeat its repertoire, but the wirelesss produced new material without end.

Leaving the listening side of entertainment and concentrating on the looking aspect, you might well find the domestic version of the seaside 'what-the-Butler-saw' machine. These were based on a series of consecutive images flicked past a viewing aperture, and came under the name of Kinetoscopes (152) or even Filoscopes. They were common in the 1890s and were often sold with sets of interchangeable subjects, the more ornate versions having a crank handle to turn the pictures round. The Praxinoscope (153) also played on the phenomenon known as 'persistence of vision', which allows the brain to read a continuous moving picture from several static ones. Patented by Reynaud in 1877, it had a hand-cranked drum faced with mirrors, one for each image drawn. The distance between the drawings and the mirrors was such that the image was seen on the axis of the drum and so always appeared in the same place.

It was not a far cry to cinematography but although there were hand-cranked portable models such as the Gamage of 1913 (150), home movie projectors were not to become domestic gadgets for another fifty years. For more constant pictures there were magic lanterns (148,149), such as the 'Optimus', usually with only one lamp and taking a single transparency at a time. The light source was either an oil lamp, a carbon arc or later an electric light bulb, while transparencies were sold in sets telling a familiar story. For the more adventurous, there were two-tiered lanterns which allowed one lamp to throw a background image while the other one projected a movable picture. Needless to say the success of the entertainment lay in the projector operator's talent as a storyteller.

Another popular item was the stereoscope for looking at pairs of photographs. The principle of the stereopair was first noted by Sir Charles Wheatstone in 1832, and was based on the making of two different pictures, each one seen from a few inches apart—i.e. the distance between the eyes, and then viewed together at the same time. Stereoscopes had their hey-day in the 1850s and 1860s and then again from 1890 to 1910, though the 'Holmes' stereoscope (151) dates from around 1885. As most of the photographs were mounted on to card backings, stereoscopes had either open tops or mirrors to admit light on to the scene. Less frequently, the stereo transparencies were made on glass, or else on thin paper, and hand tinted from behind. To view these, the stereoscope had to have a ground glass screen behind the images. Photographs were sold in sets, the most popular subject being travel.

It took some time before moving pictures were common in the home. In fact there was nothing to receive because regular television broadcasts were not to begin until 1936 although on an experimental basis transmissions were made by the BBC from 1929 onwards. These were on a 30-line as compared with our present 625-line picture, so the image quality left much to be desired. Receivers designed by John Logie Baird called Televisors were on sale in 1930 for 25 guineas, though the picture was only 2 × 3 inches, and in a 'portrait' format rather than the later 'landscape' convention. In those days the future of television did not exactly look rosy and yet today it must be the most common household appliance of all.

The desk

And what of the other side of the coin? Not all the hours of the day were devoted to leisure. Work too had its role. When a house was not large enough to have a separate study, the alternative was to work at that item of office/domestic furniture, the bureau, with its roll down top and chest of drawers all in one. There you would find the pens and pencils, note-paper, bills and letters (*154–163*).

Fountain pens, as we know them, were the invention of the American Mr L. E. Waterman, who in 1884 succeeded in producing a pen with an ink reservoir and a controlled ink flow. Lead pencils became cheap and widespread after 1895 when electric arc furnaces began to produce the graphite by electrolysis. But the real gem of the desk was the typewriter. Developed as an office machine by Christopher Scholes and Carlos Glidden of Milwaukee between 1866 and 1873, it was first manufactured by E. Remington and Sons from 1874. You may notice a similarity of artistic embellishment in early sewing machines but this is no accident. In manufacturing terms, Remingtons had gained a lot of experience from over a decade of making sewing machines and it was logical to use the same skills in their new product. Selling at $125 and writing in capital letters only, the typewriter took a few years to become accepted, though success was finally achieved after Remington had proved its value by lending

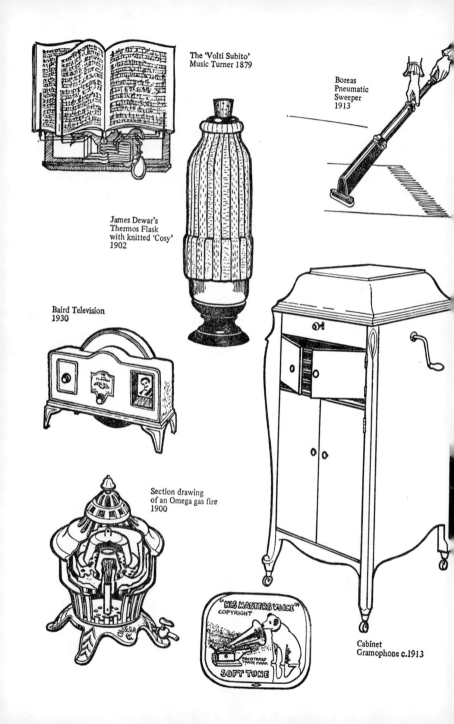

The 'Volti Subito'
Music Turner 1879

Boreas
Pneumatic
Sweeper
1913

James Dewar's
Thermos Flask
with knitted 'Cosy'
1902

Baird Television
1930

Section drawing
of an Omega gas fire
1900

"HIS MASTERS VOICE"
COPYRIGHT
REGISTERED
TRADE MARK
SOFT TONE

Cabinet
Gramophone c.1913

machines to companies in America. By the end of the century the typewriter found a place in the home of those who, like writers, ran their businesses from there. Models such as the 'Merritt' (*163*) and the 'Peoples' Typewriter were built in a less robust manner and consequently were cheaper than the more common office machine to try and entice the average customer. At only £5, you could afford to be average.

On the desk there might also have been the table fan, though of course not before the development of the electric motor. They were first made in 1882 by the Crocker and Curtis Electric Motor Company of New York and their main function was to cool you down, a necessary convenience for those stifling air-less summers of New York. Mains (*165*) and battery models (*166*) were made with black japanned stands and brass blades. The makers of 'Ever Ready' batteries in 1900 advised the customer not to buy more than one spare set of batteries because 'they exhaust whether in use or not', so it was better to buy the slightly more expensive mains model and plug it into the light socket. By 1900 fans as made by the Improved Electric Glow Lamp Company were on sale in London from 3 guineas. They had three speeds and could be tilted and turned in any direction—in fact almost guaranteed to blow all the papers off the desk!

Having just stated that the fan was dependent on the electric motor, there is always the exception to the rule. There was a hand-powered model (*164*) rather like a toy windmill on the end of a pair of curling tongs. It had a small ratchet and fly-wheel and was operated by squeezing the two handles together. The maker's boast of 2,800 revolutions per minute was a clear case of wishful thinking, particularly as the entire apparatus weighed only 5 ounces. Nevertheless, it was claimed to be 'useful' against flies, gnats and mosquitoes and for drying the hair after a shampoo—a particularly dangerous suggestion as there was no protective wire frame over the blades.

Sewing machines

The name we associate with the sewing machine is that of Isaac M. Singer of Boston, Mass., who built the first practical domestic model in 1858, though he had produced an industrial model in 1851. Singer was not the first man to make a lock-stitch sewing machine. In fact in the same state of Massachusetts, Elias Howe had patented a machine in 1846 but it had certain impracticalities which Singer overcame, notably that the fabric had to be pinned to a plate which passed under the needle. Each time the length of the plate had been sewn, the fabric had to be unpinned and moved along, and by this method could only be sewn in straight lines. Singer left the fabric free which allowed it to be turned in any direction, and what was more important, the needle went up and down and not from side to side like Howe's model. That meant the weight of the material rested on the bed of the machine, rather than hanging from the side of it by pins. It was clearly a much better method and the one which is still used today.

Singer's 1858 lightweight domestic machine called the 'Family' was followed in 1865 by a more robust 'New Family' model (*168*), and in order to increase sales was sold in an entirely new way. The company introduced what has now become a familiar system known as Hire Purchase which effectively allowed the user to pay for the machine by selling the end products as they were made. Of all household gadgets, the sewing machine was the first complex machine to be made for the home, and paved the way for the host of other intricate appliances which blossomed in our period of 1860–1930.

There were many rival sewing machine manufacturers but they basically followed the same pattern, a machine with a long over-hanging arm, a hand-turned crank for fine control and the foot treadle in a cast iron frame for rapid sewing. It came with a wooden cover, ideally suited for sitting on while working the machine (the shape and construction of which, incidentally, also became a familiar part of the later phonograph). Of the many rivals, here we include the Lancashire-made model by the still extant Jones company (*167*) dating from *c.* 1880. By this date machines had the automatic fabric advance mechanism and bobbin winder. The exaggerated decorations and styling of the late nineteenth century was given free rein in the sewing machine, as the 'Royal Anchor' model (*169*) of 1871 will testify. The shape of the anchor, complete with coiled rope serves no function at all, and the upper arm is quite useless, except for carrying;

but then with a solid cast iron machine on a heavy cast iron base, who would want to move it any more than was absolutely necessary? Made by Thomas Bradford of London and Manchester (the company that also made washing machines and mangles), the Royal Anchor sold for £5. Less ornate, but still boasting the flowery transfers, is the chain-stitch machine of Willcox and Gibbs (*171*), this model dating from the mid-1890s, from a company who had been making sewing machines since 1856.

The sewing machine did much to further the 'American System' of manufacture, that of mass-produced interchangeable parts. By the end of the nineteenth century the method was well proven, and American supplied and owned companies were being established all over the world. Singer's factory at Clydebank in Scotland produced 13,000 sewing machines a week, which kept prices low and sales high (note the Atlas Organ Company of Camden Town's sewing machine at £1/19/– mentioned on page 38). Keeping prices really low, tiny hand-operated models had appeared in the late 1850s which had to be clamped to the table top. Joseph Hendrick's sewing shears of 1858 resembled a pair of scissors and used the same motion to move the needle up and down.

The advantage of owning a sewing machine was that it allowed the family to get longer service out of household linen by facilitating durable repairs, to alter clothes as children grew up, and to make new clothes according to the latest fashions. The latter would have been inconceivable without a good dressmaker before unless one had a tailor's dummy (*172*). At the turn of the century these were known as French Busts; one company that used to make them is still in business, though they now make shop-window mannequins and wax figures for museums. The dress stands were adjustable to match the maker's figure and could have a bustle appendage as the fashion demanded.

The dining table

As already mentioned, the term 'Living Room' as used here, covers a variety of functions not the least important being that of dining. The gadgets that are associated with the dining table are usually somewhat of a status symbol, for otherwise they would have remained hidden below stairs. In this category we include toasters, coffee-makers and the like.

The breakfast table might boast a few gems. For instance, if the master was having boiled eggs before his kippers, mushrooms, kidneys and sausages, then the table would be laid with an extra item of cutlery—the egg topper (*173*). The German version which was also copied in America, resembled a pair of scissors decorated to look like a cockerel. One blade was a round flat knife, while the other was an open circle which fitted over the egg. The model illustrated was made by Messrs Fisher in 1904. The standard American and English model was designed more on the nutcracker principle, but with spikes facing inwards ranged round two semicircles. They pierced through the shell and part of the way into the egg white when the two hinged halves were squeezed together. Both versions were common by the turn of the century though there were many designs patented during the seventy years covered in this book. Most of them were frighteningly complicated and it is doubtful whether they ever graduated from an inventor's dream to being a common gadget.

Another gem was a self-pouring tea pot (*174*). John Royle of Manchester patented this oddity at the turn of the century. It was basically a tea-pot with a plunger which, when pushed down, displaced the tea, forcing it up the spout. No lifting or tipping was required. One of the few variations of adding boiling water to tea-leaves was dreamed up in Edison's Electric Appliance Company, New York, in the 1920s. The forerunner of the tea-bag, Edison's 'Hotpoint' Electric Tea Infuser was, in effect, an ornate electric kettle. It came with a perforated metal canister attached to the tea pot lid which could be filled with tea and then suspended in the water after it had boiled. Once sufficiently infused, the canister could be raised and fixed out of the water in the hollow of the lid. For the most part, however, there was little tampering with the time-honoured art of tea-making, unlike the vast range of coffee-making devices.

The making of coffee still has something of the ritual about it, perhaps because it is easier to make a bad cup of coffee than a bad cup of tea. Coffee has been drunk in the West since the early seventeenth century, using the Turkish method. Still one of the best ways of making coffee, this required roasting the beans, grinding them to a fine dust and adding an equal quantity of sugar and coffee to the top of an individual-sized brass pot of cold water. Over a fire the pot was brought to the boil without stirring, and then removed from the heat at the last moment just before the whole thing boiled over. Then it was stirred, poured into a cup and allowed to settle. The result was a thick sweet black brew, a third of which was mud at the bottom of the cup. The limiting factor was the size of the pot and hence portion, and the thick deposit. Clearly there was a need to make larger quantities of coffee without the grounds, the simplest answer being to decant the coffee through a filter into another larger pot below. Some people made coffee by putting the fresh grains into the upper filter portion, and pouring boiling water through, but this made a weak drink because there was not enough time to extract the flavour. The answer lay in the percolator (*178*), invented by Count Rumford in 1806. This had a fairly narrow inner container with a filter that sat low down in a larger container. Water trickled through the coffee and then surrounded the perforated container letting the strength increase by infusion. The inner section could then be removed at the desired strength and the coffee served. Rumford's percolator also boasted a water-jacket which could be filled with boiling water to keep the coffee hot. If you were worried that some of the grounds might come through into your cup, then you could fix a 'Standard' strainer which hung on the outside of the spout. In nickle-plated brass, this patented design of 1890 sold in New York for 25 cents.

More of a conversation piece was the Napierian Coffee Machine (*179*) which worked on the principle of expanding and contracting steam. It came on a stand, complete with a spirit burner and two separate containers. The first one was glass and filled with water. This was connected by a pipe to a second vessel in china or bronzed copper, which had the coffee grains in the upper section. On boiling, the water expanded into steam, was forced up the pipe and through the coffee into the pot below. Resembling a chemistry laboratory experiment, the Naperian made spectacular bubbling and spluttering noises while it worked. For effect it was only surpassed by the Cona coffee-maker which had two glass bowls one above the other, water in the bottom, coffee grains in the top. The water was boiled by a spirit lamp, taking about 20 minutes for 1 pint, and then forced up a central pipe, through the coffee and into the upper vessel. If the lamp was removed shortly after the water began to rise, the rest of the liquid would continue to be forced up the spout by the expansion of the steam. After much bubbling, for a while all would be quiet while the coffee was infused, but during this time the lower bowl was cooling down and the steam condensing. This created a partial vacuum which sucked the coffee back down aided by the weight of atmospheric pressure above—all principles understood and used in the workings of early steam engines. Perhaps because of its spectacular visual performance, the cona method has remained popular.

'Here's a hint for those who like good coffee at home but cannot get it,' ran an article in the *London Illustrated News* of 1910: 'Try the Caffeta Coffee Maker (*177*) . . . you just place the coffee and water together in the machine, light the lamp, and wait till the whistle blows. Delicious fragrant coffee is then at your disposal. The machine is air-tight and does not let the coffee stew, or boil—which means spoil: it just lets it come to the boil.' At 25/- for the eight-cup model, what more could you want? It had one slight drawback; if by chance you weren't in the room when the whistle went, you did allow the water to boil despite what the advertisement said. The machine was only air-tight as long as the whistle was not blowing, and in this way was in effect a small pressure-cooker and if left unattended would firstly ruin the coffee and secondly probably blow up.

To keep your bristling Victorian moustache out of your cup you only had to clip on one of Donaldson's Detachable Moustache Guards (*176*) . . . if you happened to have a particularly difficult growth that would get in the way, back in 1895!

Still at the breakfast table, we might expect to see the toaster and its forerunner, the toast crisper (*175*). Bread was toasted on the end of a long fork in front of the fire grate, or if you were the proud owner of a gas cooker, under the grill. But once it came to the table, it would quickly become soggy unless kept under a toast crisper. This miniature oven had its own spirit burner and a hood to contain the heat, and sold in 1904 for £4. Electric toasters were on sale by 1920, and apart from having open sides and no 'pop-up' facility, used the same basic heating element as their modern counterpart, i.e. bare wire wound round flat mica sheets. Bread could be held against either side of the G.E.C. 'Magnet' toaster by the spring-loaded sides. When opened the bread slid down and aligned itself with the untoasted side facing the heating element so the second side could be done. The 'Universal' (*185*), an American model of 1923, by Landers, Frary and Clark, held the bread in a special cradle which could be slid against the element to toast either the left or right side. Like many early electrical gadgets, toasters were not earthed.

In the evening after supper, the dinner guests might adjourn to the sitting room for coffee, brandy and cigars, and here we would expect to find all the gadgets that go with that form of relaxation. The soda siphon, for example, has been made since Dr John Nooth's (or North) apparatus was invented in 1775. Sodium bicarbonate and flavouring such as tartaric acid was put in the upper globe and water in the lower. The top was screwed down and the whole thing tilted, allowing water to mix with the powders. This evolved carbon dioxide which dissolved in the water, and due to the pressure, forced the liquid out through the spout whenever the valve was opened. Known as the Gazogene or Selzogene (*181*), the better models came complete with their own fitted drip-tray. The glass bottle was encased in a basket of wire mesh in case of explosion. To give an idea of the popularity of mineral waters, the firm of J. Schweppe, which began in London in the late 1790s, paid £5,500 in 1851 for the permit to run the four large refreshment rooms at the Great Exhibition. During the twenty-three and a half weeks that the exhibition ran, they sold 1,092,337 bottles of mineral water (soda water with various syrup flavourings).

By the beginning of the twentieth century the 'Sparklet' Syphon (*182*) was common. Rather than mix water and powders, the company, which still exists today, offered their 'Sparklogene' for sale. It was a heavy glass bottle with the familiar wire basket which you filled with tap water up to the red line. It had a screw-on soda siphon top, but instead of mixing the chemicals, you screwed in a small cylinder containing compressed carbon dioxide. A metal spike punctured the diaphragm on the end of the capsule and allowed the gas to mix with the tap water. They sold for as little as 2/– in 1907 and the Sparklet bulbs were 1/4d. per dozen. There was even a felt-covered bottle available for use in the tropics which could be kept cool by soaking the cloth.

If you really wanted to impress your guests, you took a candlestick which had an electric light bulb in place of the candle, and placed it with much ceremony on the table-cloth, where it would suddenly light before everyone's eyes. Of course, you could only do this if you were the proud owner of one of Cooper's Electric Illuminating Cloths. First on sale in 1902 these were double-skinned green baize table-cloths of about 4 feet long by 2 feet wide, in the middle of which was sewn a pattern of electrical wires. The special candlestick had two small sharp pins protruding from its base which went through the baize and made the connection. For the best effect, the cloth was put under an ordinary table-cloth to hide it. Needless to say, like the toasters, the cloth was not earthed and the dangers of spilling your after-dinner drink can only be guessed at.

The Automatic Crystal Fountain (186), like Cooper's Illuminating Cloth, served no useful purpose other than to entertain. A fountain of liquid rose into the air and fell back into the dish below. From there it drained down the left-hand tube via a valve into the lower bulb. When the fountain stopped you turned over the bulbs like an hour-glass or egg-timer and the water was forced, partly by gravity, partly by capillary action, up the right-hand tube and out through the fountain. If you so desired, the liquid could be coloured or even perfumed.

The variety of shapes in corkscrews (180) and bottle-openers is a little bewildering, and many of the more obscure designs would pass unrecognised today if it was not for well illustrated catalogues to put us right. Naturally the kitchen had a corkscrew with a brush attach-ment, while the butler had a proper bench-mounted cork-puller in the cellar. But up on the drinks tray, bar or sideboard, there would doubtless have been rack corkscrews in bronzed or nickel-plated iron, a separate Schweppe's bottle-opener, and a lemon-squeezer and cocktail-shaker. The Thornhill Lemon Squeezer (183) dates from the late 1880s while Mr Gutmann's patent (187) was lodged in 1909.

3
The Bathroom and W.C.

Bathing

The bathroom is more of a twentieth-century concept with its hot and cold taps, fitted bath and hand basin. With it also goes the concealed piping, outside waste-pipe and unseen but attendant sewage system to take away the dirty water.

On Victoria's accession to the throne in 1837 there was no bath in Buckingham Palace and to have had a bathroom even as late as the 1870s meant you had to be rich and ready to keep up with the latest developments. Most people, if they bathed at all, sat in a tub in front of the kitchen fire as near as possible to the only supply of hot water. In fact the normal meaning of a bath in Victorian times was a *cold* bath or even a steam bath, with all the overtones of health and vitality associated with the rapid circulation of the blood.

A 'steam' bath taken in the home only occasionally had anything to do with steam. It was usually closer to a sauna, a hot air bath. Sitting in an enclosed box with just your head sticking out, a spirit stove filled the box with hot air causing ladies to glow and gentlemen to perspire (though not together!). The usual system was to have the heater *inside* the bathing cabinet positioned where it could not be reached if accidentally knocked over. Having been fastened in by someone else, the bather was trapped by the neck so if it was overturned there was a reasonable chance of burning the house down before the bath was over. The safer method was to have the heater outside as in Foot's Safety-First Folding Bath Cabinet (*188*) and in this model the bather could release himself. The height of the seat could be regulated and the makers thoughtfully provided a book rest. They claimed that physicians recommended their cabinets for the cure of rheumatism, colds, influenza, kidney, blood and skin diseases. And they only cost 35/-.

Before the days of the constant hot-water supply and built-in bath the limiting factor of a bathtub was its weight and capacity. After all someone had to fill it up with water drawn from a tap which could be some distance away, and having filled it up would at some stage be expected to empty it again. There was also the consideration that if you were actually going to have a *hot* bath then there might not be enough kettles in the house to cope. So in much of the nineteenth century you would find hip baths and shower baths, both taking a manageable quantity of water without allowing the bather to lie back and wallow. There was not enough room for his legs to fit in the hip bath so they dangled over the front edge, while his elbows were supported on arm rests on each side. The finish was brown japanned (paint) on the outside and either plain white or fake marble painted on the inside.

The shower bath was about 3 feet in diameter and a little over 6 inches deep with a metal framework above it holding the shower head. The bath would be filled with water which would then be pumped up to the top by hand, the same water recycling as long as someone remained pumping. Another system was to provide your own support for the shower head by wearing a flexible model round your shoulders (*193*). If you could be persuaded of the value of frequent cold baths, then there was an interim stage before the fully plumbed hot bath of the 1880s. What you needed was a permanent bathroom complete with a cold tap and a waste-pipe. As the proud owner of such a status symbol (which was doubtless in a converted bedroom, betrayed by the way the ornate cornice moulding on the ceiling disappeared into a blank partition wall) your shower bath was run from a header tank in the attic and so required no hand pumping. At least not for the bather. A servant would have to pump from the kitchen for about half an hour each morning to fill the tank, a task that mercifully ceased once mains water pressure was sufficient to do the job for you. For a really invigorating shower there was a knob marked 'douche'; instead of the water coming through the perforated rose, a veritable deluge poured down through a central hole about an inch in diameter. It was like standing under a fireman's hose in the privacy of your own home.

By 1865 city improvements were on an organised footing and the laying of drains, sewers, gas mains and the like went on disrupting traffic in all major centres. Electricity mains caused the same havoc from 1899 when power stations like Deptford were opened with enough capacity to serve the whole of London. The more efficient sanitary services did much towards the prevention of diseases and lowering of the infant mortality rate. A preference for hot baths emerged in this relatively molly-coddled society and the procession of servants carrying buckets of hot water from the kitchen to the tub became a feature of everyday life in the following years. Those water tanks and back-boilers in the kitchen ranges of 1860 (see page 3) provided the supply until the arrival of the geyser in 1868. Benjamin Waddy Maughan halted that procession with his invention by allowing the water to be heated right next to the bath. In his geyser (*190*) water entered at the top and filled a chamber, from where it trickled down wires getting closer and closer to the gas flames below, finally emerging at the bottom piping hot. There was no flue on the geyser so the bathroom was filled with obnoxious and dangerous fumes, and the water was contaminated by coming into contact with the waste gases. Later geysers like the 'Royal' of 1884 (*191*) kept the water separated from direct contact with the flames and by the turn of the century they even had flues.

There were other ways of heating bath water—a French method which amounted to building a fire *in* a bath, and an English one, building a fire *under* a bath. In the French one a charcoal fire was lit in a deep pot which had an air intake at the end of a tall tube and also a tall chimney for the smoke. In this way a fire could be burning inside the pot although most of it was below water level. From cold such an exercise must have taken a couple of hours to heat the water sufficiently. The English way was just as slow because it turned the bath into a glorified kettle. Available in the 1860s, these tin baths (*192*) were sold with a built-in gas burner below the tub which was swung out to be lit and then swung back in to heat the water. Being an open-topped bath the water must have cooled down almost as fast as it was being heated up.

One of the obvious consequences of the geyser was the increase in the size of baths. This in turn meant they were virtually immovable and so led to the bathroom existing in its own right, a purpose-built room in a new house rather than a corner of the bedroom. The manufacturers who were iron-founders, thought their baths may as well look nice and so produced designs with decorated cast feet and a variety of painted finishes (*193–196*). The common cast iron bath of 1880 sold at around £4 with a japanned brown outside and white inside, or up to £5 for fake wood grain and fake marble. Ornate painted models started at about £8. To maintain the *status quo* you could also have the model built into a cabinet made of deal (a very fashionable and expensive timber in 1880), oak or mahogany. It would include a fitted shower cabinet over one end of the bath, concealed plumbing and a row of taps—and all for £75, the equivalent of a plumber's annual salary! The row of taps would be '*plunge*' to let water into the bath through the hole nowadays filled by the plug; '*shower*' serving the rose at the top; '*douche*' if the shower head had one of those wide central orifices; '*spray*' for a horizontal shower from the side walls of the shower cabinet; '*waste*' which was a push/pull knob working a valve allowing the water to flow away; and '*hot*' and '*cold*' serving all the various taps. That £75 was well spent. It included any built-in ceramic tiles and also a ceramic bath tub. Cast iron was far too common and besides it needed regular repainting, while ceramic on the other hand had a superior finish which it would keep. The tub was 2 inches thick and held together with strong iron hoops and must have been more difficult to carry than a piano.

With hot water in the bathroom at the turn of a tap (and perhaps the light of a match), the gentleman's daily shaving routine was quite a civilised affair. The only other requisite for a comfortable shave was a sharp razor. The cut-throat has remained little changed for several hundred years and was made of fine hollow ground steel and usually set in an ivory or bone handle. A slight departure from the time-worn technique of slicing away stubble with that murderous instrument started in the 1880s when shorter blades were inserted into a holder but still with only one cutting edge. It meant a more even use of the steel and of course was a simpler shape to manufacture and so cheaper. To encourage rotation of blades it was not uncommon to find a shaving set including a handle and strop and blades inscribed 'Monday', 'Tuesday', etc. on their spines, a different one for each day of the week. The Kampfe Safety Razor (*197*) was of this type, patented in America in June 1880 and again in England in March 1887, and so too is the Rolls Razor (*203*), though the latter model did not offer so many blades. The electric shaving pot (*201*) was made by Merry-weather's, a firm whose main products were fire engines and fire-fighting equipment, though they also made domestic appliances.

In 1895 a man with the improbable name of King Camp Gillette from Wisconsin developed the idea of the wafer-thin two-edged blade, but had to wait for technology to catch up with him before it could be manufactured. It took until 1903 before his dream became a reality though the logic of his invention was not shared by the public, the annual sales amounting to no more than fifty-one razors and 168 blades. Gillette was working on the premise that you should use the blade once and then throw it away, but after generations of re-sharpening blades the users were at first a little sceptical. However, in 1904, they accepted the principle and decided the idea was quite reasonable, increasing Gillette's sales that year to 90,000 razors and over 12,400,000 blades (*199*)! Other manufacturers devised methods of resharpening the disposable blades, among which we include Wilkinson's (*202*) and Drew's (*204*) and by 1930 the 'Valet' Autostrop (*200*). The first electric shaver was marketed by Schick in 1931, though wet shavers still led the market thirty years later and patent blade resharpeners were still being developed in the early 1960s.

I am reminded of the contents of the bathroom cabinet by a letter received from Mr Panter who was born in 1888 at Bangor in Wales. He remembered that his father had worked with explosives and had by chance got some cordite mixed into the decorative edges of the Father Christmas outfit. Passing too close to the candles on the tree, a sleeve began to smoulder and so he tried to slap out the flame but in this way provided the necessary percussion to blow the stuff up. There being no doctor to hand his wife 'blew opium soaked in brandy down his scorched throat, which saved his life'. Few housewives are able to lay their hands on such homely remedies today. Other standard medicaments were Bile Beans, which were boasted in 1900 'To keep you Healthy, Happy and Slim'. For those who do not remember them, they were a laxative. Beecham's Pills were also a valuable stand-by. Their slogan at the same period was 'None so blind as those who won't see; none so ill as those who won't take BEECHAM'S PILLS'. Aspirins in powder form were available in Germany from 1899 on prescription, and over the counter in packets of twenty from 1915 onwards.

For brushing the teeth (*206–209*) you could choose a variety of dentifrices including solid blocks, powders and pastes. Around 1875 solid paste came in shallow pottery or glass jars perversely known as 'boxes', dentists buying blank cakes from the wholesaler and having their own names and addresses stamped on the top. Toothbrushes were then moistened and rubbed in the cake creating a lather in much the same way as the shaving-stick did. Rose, cherry or peppermint were the standard flavours available. Other boxes were made of tin, wood or pink cellulose. This, the first plastic, was made as early as 1870 and used for items such as shirt studs, collars and denture plates. By 1900 it began to replace the ivory handles of toothbrushes, the bristles still being inserted by hand until mechanisation followed in the 1920s. The price of the plastic toothbrush then fell to 6*d*. Beecham's Tooth Paste tubes resembled artists' oil paints, made of unpainted metal with a printed paper label bearing the trade-name. They were first available in 1892. By 1905 such exotic brands as Oraline and Zepto were on sale as well as the still available Colgate and Gibbs. Toothpowders were claimed to be 'composed of only the finest and purest materials' usually unspecified, but for the most part precipitated chalk. Other ingredients were hinted at in the brand names: Wood's Areca Nut toothpowder, Camphorated Chalk toothpowder, Calvert's Carbolic toothpowder, and Calox—the oxygen tooth-powder(?).

Sir William Thomson who became Lord Kelvin was one of the distinguished members of the Physical Society of London, founded in 1874. As well as his work in the development of scientific precision instruments he also designed more prosaic items such as his patent water tap (*205*). It is shown with a 'Kaver' hydraulic-powered toothbrush attachment (*206*), the forerunner of the modern electric equivalent. With prongs gripping the inside of the tap, tightened by the knurled nut below, it diverts the water through a small turbine. The water then pours back out and into the sink about an inch to the right of the tap. The rotary motion of the turbine is transmitted along the flexible cable and makes the toothbrush head twist rapidly backwards and forwards, no doubt to the joy of the bleary-eyed and pyjama-clad early riser.

Water closets

As early as the 1770s, two separate patents were taken out for flushing water closets, one by Alexander Cummings in 1775 and the other by Joseph Bramah in 1778, the latter being an improvement which was still on sale over a hundred years later.

In 1851 George Jennings, a man who had always been a campaigner for better sanitation, persuaded the committee of the Great Exhibition to allow him to install paying toilets at the Crystal Palace at his own expense. As a measure of their success he received a net profit of £1,790 and recorded that no fewer than 827,280 people used them. Continuing his service to the public, he was responsible for the underground public lavatories dotted around the city of London which he called 'Halting Stations', the first one opening in 1855 outside the Royal Exchange. At 1*d*. a visit, the price remained unchanged from 1855 to 1971, surely the all-time winner of counter-inflation. It is to George Jennings that we owe the phrase 'spending a penny'! The names of Victorian water closet manufacturers explain other pseudonyms—Edward Johns and Thomas Crapper.

Not every house had a link to the sewers so the common practice was to have a wooden seat with a hole in it directly over a cess-pit, the contents being removed at weekly or monthly intervals by 'Night Soil Men'. In our family home in the Black Forest the old house still has two such toilets, one on the ground floor and the other on the first floor, almost directly above it, the drop to the pit being about 25 feet. In 1860 the Reverend Henry Moule, the vicar of Fordington

Cabinet Lavatory
1898

The Rev. Moule's first Earth Closet
1860

Kropp Razor

Adjustable Baby Chair
1913

Coca Cola
1905

Schweppes
1886

Desk letter-holder

Mrs. Ba... lls
18 Elmlee Road
Knutsford
Cheshire

in Dorset, patented an earth closet operated by a pull handle which sprinkled a quantity of earth or ashes on to the contents of the bucket. It was certainly less smelly than the plain hole and pit system, though a long way from perfection. The model illustrated (*210*) dates from an improvement to Moule's patent taken out in 1873, and was still advertised by the Army and Navy Stores in 1908 for 30/-. Using the same seat but with a different 'fuel', the 'Triumph' Peat Dust closet appeared in an 1894 advertisement and claimed to be far superior to earth and ash closets. 'Cheaper and Nicer. No Dirt. No Smell . . . The best for Country Mansion and Cottage.'

In 1870 T. W. Twyford of Hanley noted that in assembling 'Bramah' pattern water closets he was being paid 2/- for the pottery pans while the brass and iron-founder was receiving around ten times that amount for the valve mechanism and supports. As a result he designed an all-ceramic water closet of the washout pattern, that is with the main outlet at the front of the bowl rather than at the base and an overhead cistern with the necessary valves. Tasteful decorations were the order of the day, either using transfers outside and inside the bowl, or using complex relief moulding during the casting process. George Jennings' plunger-type water closet of 1876 (*212*) was a hybrid of mechanical valves and all-ceramic bowl and is shown here without its covering seat, which resembled Rev. Moule's earth closet.

The system that is in widespread use today, the washdown closet, was invented in 1889 by D. T. Bostel of Brighton, the 'New Humber' (*214*) by McDowall, Stevens and Co. being an example of this type. The flowers covering the outside as well as the inside of the bowl are so delicate, it must have made people loath to use it. While on the subject of decorated bowls, there was a vogue to put images on the inside of the bedside potty, Napoleon's portrait being a favourite around 1800.

4
The Bedroom

The Great Exhibition featured some beautiful brass bedsteads, a style which was popularised by this great display and remained so throughout the rest of the century. Mattresses were usually of straw, horsehair or feathers, in ascending order of quality and lay on stout metal laths which had a slight amount of give in them. An improvement came in 1865 when the coiled spring mattress was patented, though in the early models the sleeper was protected from being spiked by a woven wire mesh which was stretched over the top of them. In 1870 the Champion Spring Mattress sold in New York at $13 for the double bed size and was claimed to be 'wholly composed of tenacious tempered steel springs'. F. C. Beach and Company who sold it even suggested it could be used straight on the floor without the supporting brass bedstead.

The wire-woven mesh was also developed into a mattress in its own right. Some were adjustable, like the bed of 1883 by Gamages (216) selling at 3 guineas. The mattress was made of diagonal double-woven hard spring wire which was tin-plated to prevent corrosion and fixed to a rail at the foot of the bed. The other end was taken up round a pole which was fitted with a handle. It remained a question of personal preference how tight you wound the tension, allowing you to sleep 'soft or hard at pleasure'.

The brass bedstead was, of course, more black iron than brass but the rods and knobs allowed for the attachment of all sorts of trivia from Christmas stockings to a variety of aids we shall cover later. But before looking at other gadgets in the bedroom we should not forget the concealed bed. This is one that folded out of a cupboard, sometimes already made up with the blankets held in place by canvas straps, and was known as a press bed (*217*). It was common by the seventeenth century and provided a spare bed for that unexpected extra guest, usually a second manservant who could not really be expected to share a bed with the housekeeper. By the nineteenth century press beds had become recognised as useful for rooms which were too cramped to turn around in with two beds, so during the day one was folded away.

Having got a bed for the night there is nothing worse than being too cold in it. The traditional antidote, the warming-pan, has been used for at least five hundred years though the last hundred of them has seen the arrival of many variations. The nineteenth century saw the widespread use of stoneware hot-water bottles, the most familiar type having the stopper placed centrally on top of a loaf-shaped bottle (*219*). This was because of the difficulty then, and for that matter even now, of making a ceramic screw fit well enough into a ceramic thread to remain water-tight. A rubber washer made all the difference, enough to allow a turn-of-the-century porcelain model like the 'Mecca' (*221*) to be used lying on its side but still with some risk. Even in the 'Marion' (*224*), an early rubber hot-water bottle, the convention of keeping the stopper upright to avoid leakage was continued. Looking very like a leather briefcase the bottle was intended to stand by itself. Some manufacturers were being bolder and making the familiar rubber 'lying down' type as early as the 1890s (*223*), but those customers who had experienced wet beds from leaking bottles were joined by the sceptics and steered well clear of the unreliable rubber hot-water bottle, preferring nice safe metal ones. Made of copper they were mostly round and flat in more or less the same shape as the faithful old warming-pan. For those who preferred to warm their bodies rather than the bedclothes, there was the anatomically shaped Belly Warmer (*218*) resembling an oversize hip flask.

In 1926 the tariffs for electricity were rationalised due to the linking up of Britain's National Grid, as set out in the Electricity Act of that year. Previously individual companies had sold their power at whatever price they felt was right, making it cheaper, for example, to run an electric appliance in Glasgow than in London. Now they were all standardised. One of the results of this was that electricity was added to the list of heat sources in the area that had previously been the domain of glowing coals or hot water. There was, firstly, a 12-inch long tubular heating element which was screwed into an ordinary hot-water bottle, having the same thread as the stopper. It was called the 'Supreme Miracle' though it must have been a miracle if it did not melt the rubber of the bottle by coming in contact with the sides or overheating the water. Secondly, though a little after the period covered by this book, there was an electric heater permanently built into a hot-water bottle. It was encased in an asbestos tube shaped to match the exterior, the patent by Mr F. S. Spooner Wates explaining that his system allowed the Electric Bed Heater to be any shape desirable. Rothermel Ltd took up the patent and produced a bakelite exterior which fully exploited this fact. They used the shape of the traditional rubber hot-water bottle. It was a bulky, uncomfortable and unfriendly bed heater, not to mention unsafe due to it not being earthed.

Electric blankers were also coming on to the market in the 1920s, the 'Thermega' Heating Pad (222) being a small one, a little bigger than a large hot-water bottle. It must have been the answer to a hypochondriac's prayer because the instruction leaflet claimed it to be 'A veritable godsend to all who suffer from rheumatism, neuritis, lumbago, neuralgia, earache, pneumonia, influenza, colds, insomnia, tennis arm and other ailments where warmth is a curative factor.'

To return to those items which were attached to the brass bedstead, Clarke's Adjustable Bed Tray (225) was a multipurpose tray which sold in 1890 for 15/–. It was intended to hold one of their 'Pyramid' lamps, either as a night light or by using a double wicked candle as a reading light. To that end, the Bed Tray came with an optional extra at 5/–, the adjustable book rest in brass. On the side of the screen round the light was a hook for your pocket-watch, but if the 15/– was too expensive, there was a 3/4d. version which bought just the Pyramid lamp (including plaster fire-proof holder, tray and glass cover), a box of eight refill lights and a japanned bent metal Watch Holder (226).

As they were obviously on to a good thing, Clarke's sold a Medicine Box attachment which fitted on to the back of the bed tray; also the Nursery Lamp Food Warmer (*227*) to straddle the candle. It allowed Nanny to keep baby's midnight feed at the right temperature and to take a medicinal nip of brandy herself without even getting out of bed. Clarke's recommended that night lights be lit at the front and back of every house as soon as it was dark to prevent burglaries, and to emphasise the point the individual candles came wrapped in paper printed with the legend 'The Burglar's Horror'!

Though the bedside table was the logical place for the candle and box of vestas, there were also special clamp-on models which fixed to the bedhead. The Arctic Candle Lamp of the 1890s (*228*) was one of these. Resembling an ordinary candle, it was in fact a hollow metal tube painted white with a smaller candle inside. As the wick burnt down so a spring pushed the candle up keeping the flame always in the same place (see page 34). For 7/6*d*. it came with an attached snuffer and a lampshade holder, the shade being to cut out the draught and stop the candle guttering. The model without the bracket but with the patent adjustable spring ends 'fastens securely in any ordinary candlestick'.

Clocks could also be attached to the bed, the type we show allowing you to tell the time in the dark by switching on a battery powered light bulb to illuminate the dial of a pocket-watch (*232*)—an electric version of Clarke's Pyramid Night Light Watch Holder. Others which stood on the bedside table used the same method, the Swiss eight-day model (*230*) in a tooled morocco leather case costing £2/19/– being almost identical to a wooden model of 1896 costing £4/10/– seventeen years earlier. The timepiece was still a standard pocket-watch, though for the short-sighted there was an Ever Ready Watch Stand in 1907 with a magnifying-glass supported in front of the dial. An alternative model acted like a mini epidiascope (*231*) which on pressing the button projected the dial on to the ceiling giving an image large enough to make it 'easily legible, even for the people with weak sight'. One hopes it had a focusing device to cope with the differing heights of ceilings.

There was no question of any of these being alarm-clocks. That was the duty of the servants, exemplified by an alarm-clock on show at the 1851 Great Exhibition which was labelled a 'servant's regulator'. Employment figures for that year showed domestic servants to be second only to agricultural workers who numbered 1,790,000 as opposed to 1,039,000 domestics, so there were plenty of them around to do the waking up.

The genteel way to start the day was to have a cup of tea in bed and by 1903 this could be done even if you had no servants to make it for you. The earliest automatic tea-making machine (229) was an arrangement of springs and levers patented by a Birmingham gun-smith in 1902 and selling at about 3 guineas. It required setting up the night before by filling the one pint kettle, topping up a spirit lamp and inserting a new match into a holder. At the prescribed hour the alarm would go off and the alarm winder key would consequently revolve. This motion was used to release a lever which drew a sheet of emery paper swiftly past the stationary match thus striking it and lighting the spirit stove under the kettle. On boiling, the bubbling water upset another delicate lever which extinguished the stove and tilted the kettle up, pouring boiling water into a tea-pot, or all over the bed if you forgot to put anything there to catch it. It also caused the alarm bell to ring once more just in case you had slept through the whole operation. The makers suggested quite rightly that the water could be used for tea, shaving or other purposes, but added somewhat hurt that it was 'in no sense a toy'. The snag was that the setting of the levers was so delicate that any light sleeper rolling over in the night stood a fair chance of activating the sequence by accident. If you did sleep through it you would then oversleep (the alarm having already gone off) and finally wake up to a cold cup of tea which had been standing for hours.

The first all-electric machine, the Goblin Teasmade, was made in 1933 and included an electric light and electric clock. The springs and levers were replaced with timers and mercury switches and as well as the final alarm ring to signify the cycle was complete, the lamp went on. Without the tea-maker, simple electric clocks were sold in bakelite housings for £2/10/– in 1932.

Some things should be done before going to bed, like tidying away clothes, hanging them up and putting the trousers under the mattress to press them, unless you owned a trouser press (234). In that case it had to be undone, the clothes carefully folded, smoothed flat and bolted in place under pressure, though one cannot help thinking the mattress must have been easier, just as good, and certainly cheaper. Shoes required shoe trees, to keep their shape, the best ones being made of boxwood or pear carved to match the shape of the foot, and hinged under the instep to make them easier to insert. But they had to be the right size and were not interchangeable with your sister's unless she happened to have the same size feet, so an adjustable shoe tree (235) was an obvious step forward.

The bedroom and the dressing room are synonymous in most houses, and the dressing table is a gathering-place for any number of gadgets. Scent sprays (233) and vaporisers were very popular throughout the second half of the nineteenth century and into the twentieth. Fashion had demanded beautiful scent containers with tiny paper labels bearing the maker's name and certainly not obscuring the fine cut-glass work or delicate craftsmanship. The spring piston, though equally as popular in the 1890s as the rubber bulb spray, gave way to the latter mainly because they were more expensive to make and perhaps not as fool-proof.

With the room filled with the fragrance of perfume, the right atmosphere was set to do battle with the gadgets which were supposed to help you keep up with the latest hairstyles. In the 1860s and 70s there was a school of thought who believed great things of electricity, though in fact they confused it somewhat with magnetism. An electro-magnetic curling comb of c. 1870 (238) came with a galvanic battery which was used to charge the teeth of the comb with electricity. The effect was to make the hair curl though there could be little hope of controlling the degree of curl, and the most likely side-effect was to attract all the hair-pins to stick to the magnetised comb. Magnetism was claimed to be a 'substitute for Medicine' and 'As lightening purifies the Air, so must Electricity purify the Blood'. From 1889 onwards, the Electric Chair proved it had an even more lasting effect.

By the 1920s electricity was being used rather better to warm and blow air in the hair dryer, the shape of the early models being noticeably similar to their modern counterparts. The dryer shown (*237*) is a German model made in aluminium with a wooden handle and could be run warm or hot. It was a far cry from 'The Princess' Hair Dryer of 1895 (*239*) which worked rather like running a hot-water bottle through your curls, though on a more solid and slightly smaller scale. Along the same lines, the Automatic Hair Waver and Curler (*240*) was heated up and inserted like a corkscrew into dry hair, held for a moment and unwound when cool. It produced more or less the same result as Hinde's Patent Curlers (*241*) except that they had to have the hair wound round them while still wet. It could have been dried with the electric dryer already described but would have been rather difficult with the Birmingham made 'Stebull' electric hairdryer of 1930 because it was too cumbersome to handle. The makers thoughtfully provided a bracket in front of the fan and recommended the hair be draped over it to be dried. Not very easy if your hair was short.

The other way of curling the hair was to use curling tongs, a scissor-like gadget with one solid arm fitting snugly into another shaped one. The usual way of heating them was with a spirit stove (*242*) which avoided making them dirty and so spoiling the hair. From as early as 1891 electric curling tong heaters were on sale and were even cleaner to use. They continued in use for many years (*243*) until they were ousted by cheap mass-produced curlers of plastic and smaller lighter electric hair-dryers.

Just in case all this hairdressing seems to be pampering the users a little it is as well to remember those Victorian bathing habits of the previous chapter with their cold-water baths and invigorating douches. In the 1890s the preoccupation with vitality invaded the bedroom as well for here was the pitcher of cold water and the hand basin, and lying beside it one of Bailey's Rubber Complexion Washing Gloves (*244*). Why people bothered rubbing themselves with one of those is beyond understanding. True the feeling was rather nice after the initial shock had died down because you were left with a tingling sensation, but what a shocking shade of red you turned shortly afterwards. All in the cause of beauty.

5

The Garden

To date Budding's lawn-mower (*245*) as early as 1830 might seem at first sight absurd because there is no appreciable difference between it and machines of a hundred years later. But the date is correct for in that year Edwin Budding, a textile worker from Stroud, patented his grass cutting machine and in it included all the main features still used today—the helical cutting blades running against a knife bar, a small wooden roller and a heavier metal roller behind geared to provide the drive to the cutter. Because his mower was a large one there was a handle at the front so a second person could help pull it along. In his patent Budding wrote 'Country gentlemen may find in my machines themselves, an amusing, useful and healthy exercise'. It was manufactured under licence by various firms including Ransomes of Ipswich from 1832, later to become a familiar household gadget with the rising popularity of tennis in the 1870s.

In the 1960s the term 'New' was used mainly in the field of detergents. In the late nineteenth century it seems to have meant lawn-mowers. Witness Ransomes, Sims and Jefferies' 'New Automaton' (*248*) of the 1890s. The 'New Excelsior' of 1874 (*247*) was a small model sold in New York, slightly better suited to the ordinary size garden as opposed to the country gentleman's estate. It only needed one person to push it, although with substantial lightening of the roller, the 24-inch 'New Easy' of 1890 (*246*) could boast the same advantage. Made by Selig, Sonnenthal and Co. in London, the company sold seven different models in all, ranging from a 10-inch cutting width at £2/10/- to their largest, the 24-inch New Easy at £6/5/-. Not to be outdone a Peterborough firm boasted eleven different sizes of their 'Godiva' in the 1895 *Country Gentleman's Catalogue*, starting with their 8-inch wide model that could be 'worked by a boy', a 10-inch one for 'a strong lad', 12-, 14- and 16-inch machines for 'a man', 18 inches for 'a man and boy', and so on through two men, a donkey, a pony and finally horses! The English machines were solidly built and from the above list it can be appreciated were heavy to work. American machines on the other hand were pared down to make them lighter and easier to use, though one sensed a certain lack of playing the game in the advertisement of 1895 for the 'Pennsylvania' Lawn Mower which read 'It will mow Grass closely and smoothly, and with half the labour of the best English machines. All sizes up to largest can be worked entirely by one man.' That was almost a hard sell particularly as the second part of the first sentence (from 'half' to 'machines') was printed in heavier type. In 1897 petrol-driven lawn-mowers (*250*) appeared simultaneously in Stuttgart and Newbury, NY, coinciding with the arrival of the new-fangled motor-car, though it was not until 1902 that the first commercial model was made in the UK—by Ransomes, Sims and Jefferies, of course, who came to Buckingham Palace in 1904 to demonstrate the machine to King Edward VII.

Spraying against pests was done the same way as today by filling a syringe with the relevant pesticide and pumping it out where it was wanted. Cooper's Patent Syringe (*249*) was the usual type, looking rather like a bicycle pump with a filling hose which went to a tank or bucket. There was also a model with a metal tank which you carried on your back like a haversack and worked the pumps by a long lever. At least that way you were not tied to the bucket and could move freely around the garden. The firm of Bickford's was another making a so-called portable pump which was also limited by the position of the bucket containing the mixture to be sprayed. It resembled the 'Baby Daisy' vacuum cleaner (see page 27), having a long handle that was rocked backwards and forwards to work a pair of suction pumps and feed a hose which had a spray nozzle. Like the early vacuum cleaners it required one person to pump and another to direct the nozzle.

It should come as no surprise that makers of fire-fighting equipment such as Merryweather's (already mentioned for another of their products on page 56) should also make garden hoses (251). They were made of cotton-impregnated vulcanised indiarubber. With the right fitting they could be connected to a lawn-sprinkler (252) of the type made in Massachusetts by the E. Stebbins Manufacturing Co. in 1887. The hose fitted on to the pipe just below the upper cog and the water flowed up through the central rose and also out along the three arms. The angle at which the water left the jets forced the sprinkler to revolve in a clockwise direction, the motion being aided by a toothed fly-wheel at the bottom.

One of the earliest garden gadgets was the shears, which had been in use in the 1820s. By the end of that decade a multiplication of the cutting action had been made possible in Scotland by Patrick Bell, the inventor of the corn-reaping machine. The forerunner of the present-day combine harvester, its main novel feature was the long cutting blade moving from side to side as opposed to Bell's competitors who had favoured a circular cutting motion. Ridgeway's Hedge Cutter of 1885 (253) is a hand-held implement with the same cutting action, the top set of blades moving backwards and forwards against the bottom fixed set.

Early lawn-mowers had their own heavy rollers at the back, explaining the need for often more than one person to pull them along. By lightening the roller the job was made easier but the quality of the lawn suffered because the roller's function had been to break down the soil to create a fine tilth, a process farmers had been using on a larger scale right through the nineteenth century. The remedy lay in using a separate garden roller usually made of hollow cast iron and filled with sand (256) or water (257) to add weight. Adding ballast before the rollers were sold caused unnecessary extra work and increased the cost of transportation so this was often done by the purchaser.

Some people find it very tiring to watch others work hard; all those gardeners labouring manfully on a hot afternoon under spades, rollers and the like. It was enough to wear one out, but if the master of the house had any sense he would be sitting in one of Ladd's Swing Chairs (254) to help him recover from his arduous role as spectator. His only problem would be to decide whether he would be even happier on the 'Hammoquette' Reclining Chair (255) that his wife was occupying. He could swing gently to and fro in Ladd's Chair but the Hammoquette followed the shape of the body because the wooden slats of the seat were supported on canvas belts. There was even an adjustable foot-rest. After all this was the 1880s. And no doubt the butler would soon appear with a tray of assorted drinks just to add one more impossible decision to his exhausting afternoon.

6

Miscellaneous

Depending where your patriotism lies, Alexander Graham Bell was either Scottish, Canadian or American. Born in Edinburgh in 1847, he was a teacher of the deaf and a recognised authority on speech therapy. When his two brothers died of tuberculosis he emigrated with his family to Ontario, and went to earn his living in Boston. It is claimed that the inspiration for his great invention came to him on a visit to his parents. In March 1876 he wrote '. . . the day is coming when telegraph wires will be laid on to houses just like water or gas—and friends converse with each other without leaving home'. Bell exhibited his new 'telephone' at the 1876 World Exhibition in Philadelphia, a centennial exhibition commemorating the signing of the Declaration of Independence. Within a year he had formed the Bell Telephone Company, but in Britain the establishment of a telephone service was hindered because the General Post Office did not want to lose the revenue from their telegraphic service to the new rival. In the early days the telephone service favoured businesses because it was charged for at a flat rate, regardless of how many calls were made during the rental period. To make it more attractive to the domestic user, around the turn of the century party lines of up to twenty subscribers were set up. Before that only the richest people would have had a telephone at home.

The original telephone was both a mouthpiece and earpiece (*258*) and had to be moved backwards and forwards during a conversation. Developments by numerous other people, including Edison, turned it into a more useful instrument, the Gower–Bell telephone being the standard wall model supplied by the Post Office in the 1880s. Unlike the Crossley Carbon Pencil telephone (*259*) with its fretted voice box you spoke into and only one earpiece, the Gower–Bell telephone (*260*) had two earpieces on the ends of 3 feet of flexible hose, the connections between subscribers being made as they were for many years through an operator at the Exchange.

Variations in style continued throughout the closing years of the century and included the Ericsson Table Model (*261*) in 1890, which is surely the most beautiful of all telephones. Immensely popular a 'modern-antique' version of it is still being sold, with the workings updated and the addition of an automatic dial. The Wall Telephone (*262*) was the type that might be found in the hall of a doctor or dentist who practised from home; the mouthpiece was thoughtfully made movable to accommodate people of differing height. The brightly polished nickel-plated Candlestick or Pedestal phone (*263*) appeared in 1901, to be followed later by a cheaper ebonite model. In the late 1920s the plastic handset became available (*264*), a lineal descendant of the Ericsson telephone, and formed the basis for designs over the next forty years. For those who could not afford their own sets the first coin-operated public call box was opened in Hartford, Connecticut, in 1889, a service not available in England until 1906.

Now the telephone has been with us for a hundred years and that wonderful convenience prophesied by Alexander Graham Bell has become to many people's minds a bugbear, one they would gladly be without for a moment's peace. Nevertheless, few would contest its enormous value and importance in our modern world.

Related to the telephone but on a smaller scale, communications inside a house had previously been made by using bell pulls to summon a servant. They had been linked by cords right through the house to a row of bells in the servants' hall or kitchen. An alternative system had been the voice pipe like those used on a ship to link the bridge with the engine room. In the house they were lead pipes built into the walls and terminating in wooden mouth pieces at suitable places. However, since the success of the telephone, the electric Bell Indicator board (*265*) had outdated both these types. You could even have internal telephones which ran off a battery rather than simple bell pushes but these were obviously much more expensive. Unfortunately for the manufacturers their arrival coincided with the era of the ever-diminishing servant class, so the chances were that there was no one available at the other end of the phone to run the errand anyway.

The lack of servants in the early years of the new century accounted for the appearance of other gadgets like the 'Norton' Door Check (267), a self-closing device worked by a piston and spring which closed the door for you. Similarly, with fewer servants to make up all the necessary fires, it was simpler to keep at least one room comfortable in winter by hanging a curtain over the door. If it was hung from a Portière Rod (268) then it would open with the door, some models even raising the curtain as the door opened, allowing a generous amount of fabric to lie on the floor cutting out the draught while the door was closed.

Clarke's 'Pyramid' Lamps belong to the period a couple of decades before the servant problem became critical. Many of their products related specifically to the bedroom, though not all. This wall bracket type of lamp-holder (266) was presumably for those anti-burglar night lights at the front and back of the house (see page 63). It was a common brass fitting of the type normally used for gaslights, but by the addition of a pretty tray was suitably adapted for candles.

Though the lady of the house might have preferred it, the habit of smoking was difficult to confine to the drawing room, and wherever you smoked you would need ash-trays and matches. Charles Kingsley had written a passage about tobacco in *Westward Ho!* which W. D. and H. O. Wills of Bristol quoted on their packets of Westward Ho tobacco: 'When all things were made, none was made better than Tobacco, to be a lone man's Companion, a bachelor's Friend, a hungry man's Food, a sad man's Cordial, a wakeful man's Sleep, a chilly man's Fire. There's no herb like it under the canopy of Heaven.' Though pipes and cigars had been known earlier, cigarettes were not available until 1843 in France. In England it was some time longer before they were on sale, some of the earliest brands still being made today. Passing Cloud cigarettes were first sold in 1874, Three Castles in 1878, Woodbines in 1888 and Player's Navy Cut in 1892. An average cost at the turn of the century was 6*d*. for twenty though Ogden's Red Breast was only 4*d*. for twenty. Matches, as we have already discovered, date from 1826 and safety-matches from 1855, though book matches did not appear until 1876 when they were given away as an advertising gimmick by the Drummond Match Co. of Barbeton, Ohio.

Cigar cutters have remained unchanged for at least eighty years though the table models (*272*) are now rarer. Made in brass and selling for 5/6*d*. the cigar was inserted into one of the two holes and then the metal box was pressed down bringing the blades against the cigar end. Smokers' lamps (*271*) had long handles so they could be passed round at the table, the burners being mounted on compass bearings to avoid spilling the oil. The ordinary model had a plain wooden handle and cost 5/9*d*. but the buck-horn handle cost 55/– and an elephant tusk model was as much as 63/–. The real gem however was the electric cigar lighter (*273*) on sale in the late 1880s.

It had a heavy bronze base and a white ceramic collar into which was screwed the element. This was a tiny electric fire which glowed red hot when the lighter was lifted up and went out when it was returned to the table. The power was controlled by a button on the base which was forced down by a spring to make an electric contact. It was only the weight of the lighter which kept the button pushed up and switched off when it stood on a table. The major disadvantage was the restraining length of flex making it difficult to pass around, and the fact that if the thing was knocked over it was alight and as such a major fire hazard.

Because the children did not smoke they had to be kept occupied in other ways. When father's knee was tired out from too much dandling the remedy was to put the baby into an Exercising machine (*275*) and let it do its own work. A rather more frightening machine was the Baby Jumper and Rocking Chair (*274*). The idea was for the baby to stand up and hold on to the rail while bouncing up and down. On the other hand he could swing backwards and forwards until thoroughly exhausted, after which the remedy was to unclip the springs and rock the child gently to sleep. Not that rocking is always conducive to sleeping. Few children have fallen asleep on a rocking-horse (*276*) or for that matter grown-ups, but then perhaps Vigor's Horse-Action saddles (*278*) were not quite so much fun. They offered all the exercise of horse riding without the cost of keeping a horse, the risk of accidents or problems caused by the weather. Exercising Horses had been known since the turn of the eighteenth century and were made of wooden boards separated by springs. However, few of them came fully equipped with stirrups and saddle—side-saddle for the ladies, naturally.

The other way to stay healthy was with the 1870s craze of using electricity and magnetism to revitalise the body. This could be done with an Electro-Magnetic Garter, or the Electric Corset, Electric Curlers or even Toothbrushes. An Electro-Magnetic Belt of 1879 was claimed to 'positively cure without medicine—Rheumatism, Paralysis, Neuralgia, Impotency, Rupture . . . Ague, Piles and other diseases.' But Dr Scott's Electro-Magnetic Hair Brush (*279*) which gave 'five hundred and forty currents of electricity' even stopped 'the Softening of the Brain'! It makes one realise that the world has become a sadder place since the passing of the Trades Description Act.

Index

(*The numbers in italics refer to the colour plate illustrations. Other numbers are page references. In the text, references to colour plate illustrations also appear, in brackets, in italics.*)

165